Library of Medieval Women

Women of the *Gilte Legende*: A Selection of Middle English Saints Lives

Library of Medieval Women **ISSN 1369–9652**

Series Editor: Jane Chance

The Library of Medieval Women aims to make available, in an English translation, significant works by, for, and about medieval women, from the age of the Church Fathers to the fifteenth century. The series encompasses many forms of writing, from poetry, visions, biography and autobiography, and letters to sermons, treatises and encyclopedias; the subject matter is equally diverse: theology and mysticism, classical mythology, medicine and science, history, hagiography, and instructions for anchoresses. Each text is presented with an introduction setting the material in context, a guide to further reading, and an interpretive essay.

Already published

Christine de Pizan's Letter of Othea to Hector, *Jane Chance*, 1990

The Writings of Margaret of Oingt, Medieval Prioress and Mystic, *Renate Blumenfeld-Kosinski*, 1990

Saint Bride and her Book: Birgitta of Sweden's Revelations, *Julia Bolton Holloway*, 1992

The Memoirs of Helene Kottanner (1439–1440), *Maya Bijvoet Williamson*, 1998

The Writings of Teresa de Cartagena, *Dayle Seidenspinner-Núñez*, 1998

Julian of Norwich: *Revelations of Divine Love* and *The Motherhood of God*: an excerpt, *Frances Beer*, 1998

Hrotsvit of Gandersheim: A Florilegium of her Works, *Katharina M. Wilson*, 1998

Hildegard of Bingen: On Natural Philosophy and Medicine: Selections from *Cause et Cure, Margret Berger*, 1999

Women Saints' Lives in Old English Prose, *Leslie A. Donovan*, 1999

Angela of Foligno's Memorial, *Cristina Mazzoni*, 2000

The Letters of the Rožmberk Sisters, *John M. Klassen*, 2001

The Life of Saint Douceline, a Beguine of Provence, *Kathleen Garay and Madeleine Jeay*, 2001

Agnes Blannbekin, Viennese Beguine: Life and Revelations, *Ulrike Wiethaus*, 2002

We welcome suggestions for future titles in the series. Proposals or queries may be sent directly to the editor or publisher at the addresses given below; all submissions will receive prompt and informed consideration.

Professor Jane Chance, Department of English, MS 30, Rice University, PO Box 1892, Houston, TX 77251–1892, USA. E-mail: jchance@rice.edu

Boydell & Brewer Limited, PO Box 9, Woodbridge, Suffolk, IP12 3DF, UK. E-mail: boydell@boydell.co.uk. Website: www.boydell.co.uk

Jacobus, de Voragine

Women of the *Gilte Legende*: A Selection of Middle English Saints Lives

Translated from the Middle English with Introduction, Notes and Interpretive Essay

Larissa Tracy
Georgetown University

D.S. BREWER

© Larissa Tracy 2003

All Rights Reserved. Except as permitted under current legislation no part of this work may be photocopied, stored in a retrieval system, published, performed in public, adapted, broadcast, transmitted, recorded or reproduced in any form or by any means, without the prior permission of the copyright owner

BX 4656 .J3313 2003

First published 2003
D. S. Brewer, Cambridge

ISBN 0 85991 771 1

D. S. Brewer is an imprint of Boydell & Brewer Ltd
PO Box 9, Woodbridge, Suffolk IP12 3DF, UK
and of Boydell & Brewer Inc.
PO Box 41026, Rochester, NY 14604–4126, USA
website: www.boydell.co.uk

A catalogue record for this book is available from the British Library

Library of Congress Cataloging-in-Publication Data

Jacobus, de Voragine, ca. 1229–1298.
[Legenda aurea. English. Selections]
Women of the Gilte legende : a selection of Middle English saints lives / translated from the Middle English with introduction, notes, and interpretive essay [by] Larissa Tracy.
p. cm. – (Library of medieval women)
Includes bibliographical references and index.
ISBN 0–85991–771–1 (alk. paper)
1. Christian women saints – Biography. I. Tracy, Larissa, 1974– II. Title. III. Series.
BX4656 .J3313 2003
282'.092'2–dc21 2002015721

This publication is printed on acid-free paper

Printed in Great Britain by
St Edmundsbury Press Ltd, Bury St Edmunds, Suffolk

Contents

Introduction

Silence into Speech: Writing the Lives of Female Saints

> But just the sight of this book, even though it was of no authority, made me wonder how it happened that so many different men – and learned men among them – have been and are so inclined to express both in speaking and in their treatises and writings so many devilish and wicked thoughts about women and their behavior.
>
> Christine de Pizan, *The Book of the City of Ladies*

Christine de Pizan addressed a fundamental trend among Church Fathers and medieval male authors of vilifying women in their texts – highlighting their faults and their role in the fall of man. But out of this tradition emerged hagiography, a genre of medieval literature that captured both the religious and secular imagination and gave women a new position in society and literary culture. Saints' lives served a twofold purpose: while elevating the subject they also provided a clearer picture of what role women were expected to play and how they played it, very often in their own terms with their own voice, "for unlike many other sources of the Middle Ages, saints' lives focus a great deal of attention on women: the *vitae* are directly concerned with female roles in the church and society as well as contemporary perceptions, ideals, and valuations of women."[1] Saint Paul believed that women should be silent in their worship of God,[2] but many female saints were very outspoken in their faith, and their eloquence was used as testimony to their holiness. In this way, the Church hoped to use these women as models for saintly behavior.[3] Alcuin Blamires notes that the greatest impact was exerted by the legends of virgin martyrs, who were highest on the scale of female

1 Jane Tibbetts Schulenberg, "Saints' Lives as a Source for the History of Women, 500–1100" in *Medieval Women and the Sources of Medieval History*, ed. Joel T. Rosenthal (Athens: University of Georgia Press, 1990) p. 285.

2 Cf. Tim. 2: 11–14 (Holy Bible, Douay–Rheims version, revised by Bishop Richard Challoner, 1749–52).

3 Tibbetts Schulenberg, "Saints' Lives as a Source," p. 286.

sanctity.[4] Virgin examples were necessary because women were considered dangerous by the early ecclesiastics who felt that women excited men to sinful thoughts and were more lustful creatures, leading to "the centrality of clerical celibacy, and a male determination to defend an inherited domain of intellectual pursuits aggressively against female encroachment."[5] However, the women classed as saints and set forth as exempla illustrate that women were not seen only as the "root of evil" and "daughters of temptation" in the Middle Ages. Karen Winstead describes what she calls "the Generic Virgin Martyr" and explains that consistency of content was necessary for these saints' legends:

> To appreciate how the virgins were re-created, it is essential to understand the many features that changed little from legend to legend through the centuries. Many of the standard ingredients of virgin martyr legends are found in the accounts of most early Christian martyrs, male or female: the saint refuses to participate in pagan sacrifices, debates her antagonist, affirms the fundamental tenets of Christianity, destroys idols, performs miracles, and endures excruciating torments. What distinguishes the legends of most female martyrs from those of their male counterparts is a preoccupation with gender and sexuality. Almost all virgin martyr legends dramatize some threat to the saint's virginity. Usually that threat is directly linked to religious persecution.[6]

While there is a standard formula for these virgin martyrs, the power of their voice and their defiance is not diminished; in fact, it is heightened exactly because it became the accepted pattern. Nor should the fact that many of these lives were invented detract from their powerful presence in the collections of hagiography, because in the medieval mind, they were "historical" examples. This category is not only limited to "ryght hooly virgynes"; it includes mothers, wives, repentant sinners, and holy transvestites. Their role as icons of saintly behavior is important – considering some of the strictures placed on women's behavior in the Middle Ages – because it removes them from the traditional place as homemaker and child-bearer.

4 Alcuin Blamires, *Woman Defamed and Woman Defended: An Anthology of Medieval Texts* (Oxford: Clarendon Press, 1992) p. 13.

5 Blamires, *Woman Defamed and Woman Defended,* pp. 5–6.

6 Karen Winstead, *Virgin Martyrs: Legends of Sainthood in Late-Medieval England* (Ithaca: Cornell University Press, 1997) pp. 5–6.

Many of these legends openly defy those roles, promoting a chosen life of religious contemplation instead. The legends also show that many of the disparities in rights and freedoms were based on class and not gender, for wealthy women were much more likely and able to leave their mark on literature and history than poor women who were more concerned about feeding their families than contributing to the lasting impression of medieval society. As Joan Ferrante points out,

> Women had a role in political, religious, and cultural developments from the earliest centuries of the Christian era, not continuously or ubiquitously but frequently and consistently enough to make it clear that medieval history in any form from the Middle Ages to the present which does not include the role of women, is not true history.[7]

These legends of extraordinary men and women, including the *Legenda Aurea* of Jacobus de Voragine, its Middle English translation the *Gilte Legende*, and the *Legendys of Hooly Wummen* by Osbern Bokenham, served as examples for women, not only of obedience but defiance as well. According to Teresa Coletti, "It was precisely for the edification and pleasure of these 'honorable soureigns' that East Anglian hagiographers such as Osbern Bokenham, John Capgrave, and John Lydgate rewrote the lives of saints in the fifteenth century, making *vitae* of virgin martyrs and other holy women in particular available to the ever expanding readership for vernacular religious texts among the nobility, gentry, and urban bourgeoisie."[8] While written primarily by male scribes, these legends cast a clearer light on the diverse roles of women, not only in the early Christian society in which they were composed but also in the medieval society in which they were read.

The *Gilte Legende* was a widely circulated body of literature that reached a large audience, unlike some of the more localized hagiographies, such as that of Belgian Saint Berlind, that were intended for a geographically limited audience, usually provincial or regional. The corpus of the *Gilte Legende* includes thirty lives of female saints who fall into four basic categories: the virgin, the mother, the repentant sinner, and the holy transvestite. There have been a number of

7 Joan Ferrante, *To the Glory of Her Sex: Women's Roles in the Composition of Medieval Texts* (Indianapolis: Indiana University Press, 1997) p. 39.

8 Teresa Coletti, "Paupertas est donum Dei: Hagiography, Lay Religion, and the Economics of Salvation in the Digby *Mary Magdalene*," *Speculum*, vol. 76, no. 2 (2001) p. 343.

excellent books written on the social and religious significance of the virgin martyrs, and a number of these lives have appeared in other volumes, including translations and editions of the *Legenda Aurea*; however, the majority of the saints' legends have not been examined based on their social position as well as on their gender. Nor has a complete edition of the Middle English manuscripts been published, though Richard Hamer and Vida Russell are producing a critical edition of the *Gilte Legende* for the Early English Text Society and have already completed their edition of the supplementary material found in some *Gilte Legende* manuscripts. The virgin martyrs, while occupying the highest place in the pantheon of saints, if for no other reason than the sheer number of them, are not the only women represented in the collections of hagiography. The other categories of women saints provide a different portrait of the ideal of female holiness. Eleven of these lives, including three of the virgin martyrs, have been translated here to provide examples and illustrate the influence these female figures, many of whom were vocal and outspoken, some of whom were not, had on medieval women by providing role models for piety. I have attempted to provide a diverse selection of legends to show the variety and color of the examples presented to medieval women for their instruction and edification. Gregory of Tours wrote,

> Christ exhorts us to live after the example of the saints and to fortify ourselves by His incessant precepts. He gives us as models not only men, but also the lesser sex, who fight not feebly, but with virile strength; He brings into His celestial kingdom not only men, who fight as they should, but also women, who exert themselves in the struggle with success.[9]

These models served as a rule for women to follow, much like the thirteenth-century *Ancrene Wisse* – which instructed them how to behave and live their lives – but the *Ancrene Wisse* was primarily written for anchoresses and recluses attached to local churches and not for a general audience. The texts are completely different in content and style but their overall aim is the same: to provide clear examples of a pious life.[10] Unlike the women for whom the *Ancrene*

9 Gregory of Tours, *Life of the Fathers*, quoted in Jane Tibbetts Schulenburg, *Forgetful of Their Sex: Female Sanctity and Society, ca. 500–1100* (Chicago: University of Chicago Press, 1998) p. 1.

10 There is some critical debate over the didactic intentions of these texts, however, and whether or not they were really meant to be used as instruction manuals or examples. For further contributions to this debate, see Eamon Duffy, *Stripping of*

Wisse was written, most of the saints in collections like the *Gilte Legende* have not locked themselves away from the world in silence; many of them speak out vehemently in their own defense, their words being a key to their passion and the "holy crown of martyrdom."

The female audience for the hagiographical collections consisted mainly of monastic or noble women, both classes being in a position to be highly influential and self-reliant. Belonging to a religious community or to the nobility gave women a greater amount of independence, perhaps inspired by the legends intended for their edification "recited in their monastic choirs . . . read to nuns in chapter and in the refectory during their meals, as well as in their workrooms while they occupied themselves with various manual tasks such as weaving, sewing and embroidery."[11] The legends of women saints were part of the everyday lives of many medieval women, both in and out of the cloister. Writing about Anglo-Saxon saints' lives, Leslie Donovan explains that hagiography was an educational tool:

> The lives of women saints were a means by which the medieval church sought to shape popular understanding of women's roles within Christian culture. The facts of women's lives encoded in these texts provide evidence for understanding the history of women in Christianity, medieval religious thought, and medieval popular culture, as well as the development of women's spirituality.[12]

There were many prominent and powerful women during the early Middle Ages active as patrons of monasteries and churches as well as authors, and the hagiography reflects their influence on the social and political climate of that period: "New understandings of the role of the saints in the Middle Ages, however, have stressed the ways in which hagiographic narrative and cultic practice, far from simply representing a stable, transhistorical realm of Christian values, participated in crucial ways in the production of social and political power."[13] But the hagiographical trend shifted later in the medieval period when female saints such as Elizabeth of Hungary, one of the

the Altars (New Haven: Yale University Press, 1992); and Katherine J. Lewis, "Model Girls? Virgin Martyrs and the Training of Young Medieval Women in Late-Medieval England" in *Young Medieval Women*, ed. Katherine Lewis, Noel James Menuge and Kim M. Phillips (Gloucester: Sutton, 1999).

11 Tibbetts Schulenburg, "Saints' Lives as a Source," p. 288.

12 Leslie Donovan, *Women Saints' Lives in Old English Prose* (Cambridge: D. S. Brewer, 1999) pp. 11–12.

13 Coletti, "Paupertas est donum Dei," p. 339.

last saints included in the *Legenda Aurea*, were venerated not for being outspoken but instead for their humility and silence. Jane Tibbetts Schulenburg points out that

> In the eleventh century, economic and formal political power among women of the elite classes began to deteriorate in many regions in Europe. The Church and government attempted to move women out of public roles and to marginalize them. Corresponding to these changes, new ideals of sanctity emerged for women: with the new "privatized" domestic saint or the obedient, subservient wife-saint, for example, the Church attempted to popularize and promote passive virtues for women.[14]

But the legends of the early Christian saints, including those who were much quieter than their virgin contemporaries, continued to circulate and gain popularity, even though their message seemed contradictory. Monique Alexandre explains that while justifying a reinforcement of the traditional subordination of women, many of these texts opened up a realm of freedom.[15] Many of these "silent" saints were venerated because their defiance took a much more feasible form, like Elizabeth of Hungary who defied the conventions of her social position and family in adopting a contemplative life but did so without great speeches or vocal displays. Secular medieval writers used these female saints as examples of brave, valiant women. Christine de Pizan, in *The Book of the City of Ladies*, gives a synopsis of the lives of several popular female saints, including Dorothy, Christina, and Marina, saying that she includes these accounts "because of their constancy during martyrdom."[16] She commends them for their bravery and their opposition to the standard expectations of women, using them as examples of "good" women who do not fit the stereotype perpetuated by patristic writers like Saint Augustine and the "masculine myth."[17]

[14] Tibbetts Schulenburg, *Forgetful of Their Sex*, p. 7.

[15] Monique Alexandre, "Early Christian Women" in *A History of Women in the West*, vol. 1, *From Ancient Goddesses to Christian Saints*, ed. Pauline Schmitt Pantel (Cambridge, Mass.: Harvard University Press, 1992) p. 410.

[16] Christine de Pizan, *The Book of the City of Ladies*, trans. by Earl Jeffrey Richards (New York: Persea Books, 1998) pp. 232–4, 241. Christine discusses a number of female saints: Dorothy, III.9.2–4; Christina, III.10.1; and Marina, III.12.1.

[17] Natalie Zemon Davis, foreword to *The Book of the City of Ladies* by Christine de Pizan, p. xxxiii. For a discussion of Christina's speech and Christine de Pizan's answer to the antifeminist clerics, see Kevin Brownlee's article "Martyrdom and the Female Voice: Saint Christine in the *Cite des Dames*" in *Images of Sainthood*

The kinds of women featured in the medieval hagiography vary greatly. Though fairly uniform in its selection of male saints, the *Gilte Legende* offers a wider selection of female saints, illustrated by the selection of translations included here. The lives of women saints fall into four distinct categories, which sometimes overlap: the virgin martyr or "right hooly virgyne," holy mothers, repentant sinners, and holy transvestites. All had one common trait: they were born of noble blood, which may seem problematic in viewing these lives as exempla for ordinary women, but it was necessary to present them as ideals. In reference to Bede's female saints in his *Ecclesiastical History of the English People*, Henrietta Leyser says,

> The paradoxes and strains of Christianity which so trouble Bede's men seemingly impinge not one whit on his women. They take up its challenges with alacrity and with evident success. They become saints apace, exercising power in life and in death: in life in positions of influence as abbesses, in death through miracles worked at their shrines. Yet it is not any woman who can play this part; royal blood is an essential prerequisite. The high profile such women achieve would indeed seem to be explicable only if Christianity was in fact offering a continuation, albeit with significant variations, of roles in which aristocratic women were already well versed.[18]

These noble women took their stand and raised their voices to varying degrees based on the unique circumstances of their gender, in some cases hiding and abandoning the essence of the very sexuality that placed them on a pedestal as objects of veneration. Each category focuses on extraordinary women in extraordinary circumstances, but their examples were intended for a larger audience of women who might find inspiration in their lives. Just as women in medieval society were diverse in class, rank, and standing, and the amount of power dependent on that position, so too are the lives of female saints diverse in their position and power. The virgins are highest on the scale of sanctity (their voice is the loudest); next are the holy mothers, the repentant sinners, and at the bottom, among the meekest and most silent of women, are the holy transvestites.

in Medieval Europe, ed. Renate Blumenfeld-Kosinski and Timea K. Szell (Ithaca: Cornell University Press, 1991); and Maureen Quilligan, *The Allegory of Female Authority: Christine de Pisan's* Cite des Dames (Ithaca: Cornell University Press, 1991).

18 Henrietta Leyser, *Medieval Women: A Social History of Women in England 450–1500* (London: Phoenix Grant, 1995) pp. 20–1.

"A Ryght Hooly Virgyne"

The majority of female saints in the *Gilte Legende* corpus are virgin saints, tormented by lustful prefects who would either marry them or defile them; in either case, their virginity is threatened, and they defend it with their faith and eventually their lives. Winstead explains that this threat is essential to the pattern of female hagiography because it became the focus of their heroism and later the devotional cults:

> Not surprisingly, as the early medieval Church began to promote virginity more zealously and as monasteries became the principal centers of cultural production, virgins swelled the ranks of the female saints. Indeed, by the sixth century, the Christian heroine was almost invariably a virgin; what is more, she was almost always a pretty, young virgin with a distinguished pedigree. So compelling was this stereotype of the female saint that some legends about early Christian martyrs underwent dramatic transformations to accommodate it.[19]

This prototype reappears throughout the *Gilte Legende*; the virgin martyrs were obviously the most popular female saints included in this collection. The legends of virgin saints also contain accounts of violent and sustained torture absent from the other lives. As they refuse to wed or be defiled, their bodies are tormented and destroyed. Their virginity is a symbol of the faith they refuse to relinquish, and as their bodies are ripped apart, they become the key to their martyrdom. Gail Ashton notes that the "focus of virgin martyrology is an exemplary death rather than an exemplary life."[20] Saint Christina, Saint Dorothy, and Saint Margaret of Antioch are translated here as examples of women saints whose sanctity was contingent on the defense of their virginity. Christina is subjected to rigorous torture at the hands of her father and the judges who follow him; her breasts are cut off, her tongue cut out, her flesh torn off, and she is finally boiled in hot oil to preserve her virginity and her faith. The

19 Winstead, *Virgin Martyrs*, p. 9.

20 Gail Ashton, *The Generation of Identity in Late-Medieval Hagiography: Speaking the Saint* (London: Routledge, 2000) p. 33. For further studies on the authorization of female virginity, specifically in Anglo-Norman texts, and the representation of virgins in hagiography, see Jocelyn Wogan-Browne, *Saints' Lives and Women's Literary Culture: Virginity and its Authorizations* (Oxford: Oxford University Press, 2001).

reader is led to believe that these women would probably not have been tortured had they consented to the sexual demands made upon them; their religion plays a secondary role to the preservation of their chastity, though the purity of their bodies becomes a manifestation of the purity of their faith. Kathleen Coyne Kelly points out, in *Performing Virginity and Testing Chastity in the Middle Ages*, "This book should at least suggest (following Caroline Walker Bynum) that the dualist concept of body/mind or body/soul that we sometimes impose on the Middle Ages is just that: an imposition. Virginity and its verifications, chastity and its confirmations, demonstrate that bodies and spirits are not easily separated in medieval practice."[21] In protecting their bodies, these women were also protecting their souls. These legends give women a much louder and prominent voice than has previously been attributed to women in medieval literature. While some of the early patristic writers, like John Chrysostom, author of *On the Necessity of Guarding Virginity*, discouraged women from being outspoken, the legends of virgin martyrs rely on it. Chrysostom believed that "spiritual chastity takes precedence over its bodily analogue, and it is extremely fragile: true virginity is even endangered by verbal intercourse."[22] However, virgin saints like Agnes challenge their tormentors to do their worst:

> Agnes said, "What will you do? For you may never have what you require. I praise neither your fair words nor your menacing." . . . He could not harm her because she was nobility, only because he accused her of being Christian. She answered, "I tell you plainly that I will never sacrifice to your gods; I will never be defiled by strange filth because the angel of Our Lord is with me and is the keeper of my body."[23]

Despite Agnes' articulate defense of her religion and her body, Kelly claims that Ambrose's account, which was the primary source for this legend, "gives us not a narrative of what 'happened' to Agnes, but an abstract panegyric that focuses on her bravery and eloquence in the face of her executioner."[24] She also asserts that the

21 Kathleen Coyne Kelly, *Performing Virginity and Testing Chastity in the Middle Ages* (London: Routledge, 2000) p. 2.

22 Kelly, *Performing Virginity*, p. 4.

23 Leslie Donovan includes translations of Lucy and Agnes' legends in her edition of Anglo-Saxon women saints' lives (*Women Saints' Lives*). These passages are translations of my transcriptions from British Library MS Harley 630.

24 Kelly, *Performing Virginity*, p. 54.

threat of "menaced virginity is barely discernable,"[25] primarily because the threat of being dragged to a bordello would not have an effect on a "pure" virgin, for as long as her mind does not consent, then her body is not truly defiled. However, the eloquence of her argument serves another purpose. It highlights the ability of women to argue their faith, defying the pagan law and those who wield it, setting them up as models of piety and devotion, as well as defiance, for medieval women who were exposed to these legends.

Saint Lucy debates the finer issues of the Christian religion with Faspasian, telling him that she is bound by the ordinance of her God and, therefore, not by the laws of the pagans, and though he seeks to still her tongue by beating her, she defies him, saying he cannot silence the Word of God within her: "Lucy replied, 'You speak of the ordinance of your princes and I keep the ordinance of my God. You dread your princes and I dread my God. You would please them and I desire to please my God. You would not anger your prince and I would not anger my God. Therefore, do what you think is most profitable.' " Her chastity cannot be violated, and her flawless body is symbolic of the force and purity of her convictions:

> She said, "Those who live chastely are temples of the Holy Ghost." Faspasian replied, "I shall have you led to the bordello and there you will lose your Holy Ghost." Then Lucy said, "The body cannot be corrupted unless the thoughts consent, because even if you had me corrupted by strength, my crown of chastity will increase because it does not lie in your accursed power to bend my consent or will. My body is ready for all the torments you can devise. Why do you hesitate, son of the devil, begin the torments you desire."

Lucy, Agnes, and Christina were popular saints whose legends were reproduced for centuries. Elevating women who refused to be physically used to the level of saint and basing that sanctity on their desire to keep their bodies for themselves, or God, lends a new dimension to these legends written by men, many of whom had a certain fear of the female body, rooted in the idea that all temptation was born of Eve. Perhaps some of that fear is exercised in the way the torture of these virgins is written, focusing on the offending female parts and on the fact that their persecutors are driven by lust. Marina Warner discusses the specific torture of female saints based on their

25 Kelly, *Performing Virginity*, p. 54.

gender and surmises that it is part of the power of virginity and was used by the Church Fathers to redeem women who were tainted by the Fall; therefore "the defense of virginal state was worth all the savagery to which saints like Catherine of Alexandria (d. c. 310) submitted."[26] The female body was a mystery to the male ecclesiastics, and this led to a muted fear of women's bodies:

> An oft-noted feature of medieval women's religious experience is its bodily expression. Medieval texts regularly describe holy women, much more than holy men, as fasting, swooning, swelling, bleeding, or otherwise manifesting their interior spiritual dispositions through concrete physical signs. Women, as scholars agree, are embodied physicality in a way that men, more often identified with mind and spirit, are not.[27]

There is a live critical debate regarding the sexualization of torture and its specific use against young virgins.[28] The virgin martyrs are the most physical, as well as vocal, female saints because their bodies are the focus of their faith and sanctity. Kelly asserts that virginity was defined by the Church as a political means of controlling women and its enemies: "Chrysostom thus politicizes virginity, using it as a weapon against the perceived enemies of the Church. *De Virginitate* is a formative document in an emerging policy that makes the Christian Church the only institution with the power to define, recognize, and reward virginity."[29] She also suggests the saints represent the Church that, like the virgins, has resisted violation at the hands of pagan persecutors.[30] The authors of hagiography used the

26 Marina Warner, *Alone of All Her Sex: The Myth and Cult of the Virgin Mary* (New York: Vintage Books, 1976) p. 69.

27 Catherine Mooney, *Gendered Voices: Medieval Saints and Their Interpreters* (Philadelphia: University of Pennsylvania Press, 1999) p. 13.

28 For recent contributions to this debate on the sexualization of torture in hagiography see Katherine J. Lewis's article " 'Lete me suffre': Reading the Torture of St. Margaret of Antioch in Late Medieval England" in *Medieval Women: Texts and Contexts in Late Medieval Britain: Essays for Felicity Riddy*, ed. Jocelyn Wogan-Browne, et al. (Turnhout, Belgium: Brepols, 2000); and Sarah Salih's "Performing Virginity: Sex and Violence in the Katherine Group" in *Constructions of Widowhood and Virginity in the Middle Ages*, ed. Cindy L. Carlson and Angela Jane Weisl (New York: St Martin's Press, 1999).

29 Kelly, *Performing Virginity*, p. 4.

30 Kelly, *Performing Virginity*, p. 41. Also see: Kathleen Coyne Kelly, "Useful Virgins in Medieval Hagiography" in Carlson and Weisl, eds, *Constructions of Widowhood and Virginity.*

definition proscribed by the Church to make their female role models, particularly the virgins, beyond reproach. However, if the clerics were intent on controlling women by providing these examples, then allowing them to voice their opposition so vehemently works against them, because their speech provides an instrument of defiance, not submission.

Many of these virgins were also venerated because of their torture and torment as brides of Christ, refusing to wed a mortal man because of their marital commitment to God. Their legends are punctuated by textual examples of this union: visions of marriage beds and references to their heavenly spouse. But the virgins are not the only example of saints wedded to their Savior. Saint Theodora, a holy transvestite and repentant sinner, and Saint Elizabeth, the medieval nun who forsakes her children for her heavenly husband, join Saint Dorothy and other martyred virgins at the wedding feasts of Christ. This is the supreme expression of a saint's love for her God; she becomes wedded to him, relinquishing her family, her status, and her body to serve him.

The Symbol of Holy Motherhood

This category focuses on a much smaller group, the female saints who are mothers and express their piety in forsaking their children for the love of God. They are less vocal than their virgin contemporaries because as mothers, wives, and widows they were not considered pure, and so their sanctity must manifest itself according to their status. Many of the women are a combination of wife, widow, and mother. Widowhood was considered a holy state itself, but it is the sanctity achieved by women who denied their maternal nature and abandoned their earthly children in favor of a contemplative, spiritual life that is most striking in these legends.[31] Saint Paula and Saint Elizabeth of Hungary have been translated here as examples of these holy mothers. Paula is frequently classified as a "widow" in the studies of hagiography,[32] but her legend emphasizes the pain and struggle of leaving her children. Paula is an earlier version of Elizabeth, who renounced her wealth and family in the thirteenth century, in her own way challenging social convention. As Ferrante explains, "Virginity, of course, gave women a particular standing – it

31 For further references on medieval motherhood, see Barbara Newman's chapter "Maternal Martyrs" in *From Virile Woman to WomanChrist* (Philadelphia: University of Pennsylvania Press, 1995).

32 Alexandre, "Early Christian Women," p. 411.

lifted them above their sex and gender, perhaps above either sex, but in fact it is more often married women, widows and mothers who are singled out for special praise."[33] Saint Paula provides the clearest example of this idea of holy motherhood by leaving her children weeping on the shore as she sails for Jerusalem. Her ultimate sacrifice is her family, and her holiness is measured by the pain and suffering it causes her. Paula's biographer, Saint Jerome, describes her as "forgetful of her sex and of her weaknesses; she even desired to make her abode, together with the young women who accompanied her, among these thousands of monks."[34] She, like the holy transvestites, must reject her gender in order to transcend what patristic writers considered the stain of Eve to achieve sanctity, because she cannot win it through martyrdom. Many early writers, such as Jovinian, extolled the virtues of married love and living chastely within the bonds of marriage. However, these women came under attack from the very writers who elevated them to the level of sainthood. Jerome, writing in response to Jovinian, said he was asked to crush Jovinian and take up the challenge of proving the superiority of virginity over marriage.[35] However, Jerome faithfully records the pious deeds of Saint Paula after she becomes a widow and denies her children,[36] recognizing the enormity of Paula's decision and venerating her for it.

Women like Paula were revered as models not of motherly love and care, but of spiritual love and devotion. According to Tibbetts Schulenburg, Jerome had a particular distaste for those who fulfilled their motherly role; for him women could only achieve true salvation if they ceased to be women and made themselves more like men.[37] It is no surprise that he revered Paula for abandoning her children and taking up the severe religious life because, as he saw it, she was following the counsel of Christ: "Whoever loves son or daughter

33 Ferrante, *To the Glory of Her Sex*, p. 6.

34 Tibbetts Schulenburg, *Forgetful of Their Sex*, p. 1.

35 Kelly, *Performing Virginity*, p. 4.

36 Paula's sacrifice is different to that of Saint Felicity and Saint Julietta who watch their children die as martyrs and take solace in their death. Saint Felicity is venerated by her biographer Saint Gregory, who writes that she was "more than a martyr because she suffered seven deaths through her seven sons and the eighth in herself." She prefers to watch them die and know that they received their martyrdom before receiving her own. Saint Julietta is pleased when her three-year-old son's head is smashed by the provost questioning her, because she does not want to leave her son behind when she becomes a martyr.

37 Tibbetts Schulenburg, *Forgetful of Their Sex*, p. 213.

more than me is not worthy of me."[38] The perception of Paula and her role as a mother is shaped by Jerome's own ideas about motherhood, just as other saints' lives are constructed around other religious writers and their views on the supreme sacrifice. This may be one reason their voice is muted and not as audible as those of the "ryght hooly virgynes"; many medieval writers believed they were tarnished by their acceptance of the maternal and marital role. This stain could be mitigated, however, by the death of their husband, their rejection of their children, and their acceptance of a holy life away from further temptations of the world. But that does not imply that the authors of saints' lives wanted women to abandon their families and homes in search of a spiritual life. In many ways, saints like Paula are examples of the importance of motherhood and marriage because they are so difficult to leave behind; the greater the love, the greater the sacrifice. Neil Cartlidge discusses the importance of marriage in medieval society and compares its bonds to those of a religious vow:

> Indeed, one way of viewing this process is to see it as making marriage analogous to a religious calling . . . for in defining marriage as an absolute and lifelong commitment just like a religious vow, the Church made the participants' sense of inner consent seem particularly vital. At the same time, marriage itself served as a model for the definition of an individual's sense of religious bond.[39]

Both Paula and Elizabeth's sacrifices seem much greater and much holier when the importance of their earthly marriage is considered. Even though their sanctity does not manifest itself in terms of outspoken defiance, the choice they make is rendered more powerful by the enormity of what they are relinquishing.

The Repentant Sinner

Mary Magdalene is the most notable of these converted sinners; she is the most vocal and visible of all the female saints, owing to her association with Christ before his crucifixion and his appearance to her at the Resurrection. However, her past is not a large part of her legend and she appears to have transcended the stigma of being the sinful woman of the Gospels. She achieves redemption through her powerful actions and her vocal authority, setting a vibrant example for women for whom the purity of the Virgin Mary was impossible.

38 Matt. 10: 37.

39 Neil Cartlidge, *Medieval Marriage: Literary Approaches, 1100–1300* (Cambridge: D. S. Brewer, 1997) p. 12.

Geoffrey of Vendome wrote in his sermon "In Honor of the Blessed Mary Magdalene" in AD 1105 that Mary Magdalene, caught between fear and hope in the house of Simon Pharisee, "confesses her sins" and in doing so saves herself. She becomes an agent of redemption, a woman who "has healed not only her own wounds but those of many other sinners and who everyday heals still more."[40] Her speech becomes an instrument of salvation, for herself and for those who hear her, like the medieval preacher whose words were the road to salvation for his flock. This image of Mary Magdalene also encompasses her roles as an intercessor between humankind and God and as a medium between the Blessed Virgin Mary and Eve; she was an object of veneration for medieval women and held up as a role model because her sanctity was easier to emulate and much more practical in medieval society.

Of the other women featured in this category, Saint Thais, the courtesan, is the most striking. Thais and Mary are presented here to show the diversity of the women in this category and highlight the complexity of the medieval audience. These legends were very popular in the Middle Ages because they portray the extreme conversion of someone steeped in sin and the glaring contrast between sinfulness and repentance.[41] Thais is a Christian whore who knows her sin but must be converted to a chaste life by a monk who seeks her favors. There is no indictment of the monk for soliciting the favors of a courtesan, only praise for bringing her around to the "true way of life." In fact, he becomes her confessor and the mediator of her penance, which she serves as a recluse. While it may seem that Thais trades her independence for a meager existence dictated by men, her merits surpass those of the monk, and she is rewarded because she voluntarily changes her life when she realizes her error, not because he "saves" her. This legend takes a more traditional slant, where the salvation of a woman is contingent on the intercession of a man. However, there is a paradox in that the abbot comes to Thais to purchase her favors as a courtesan, stopping only when he discovers she is Christian, then blaming her for his sin. He seeks to punish her, perhaps to justify his own actions:

40 Jacques Dalarun, "The Clerical Gaze" in *A History of Women in the West, vol. II: Silences of the Middle Ages*, ed. Christiane Klapisch-Zuber (Cambridge, Mass.: Belknap Press of Harvard University Press, 1992) p. 33.

41 Alexandre, "Early Christian Women," p. 411.

> As the abbot turned to go, Thais said, "Father, where do you command that I put my natural waste?" He replied, "In the cell as you deserve." Then she asked how she should pray to God and he replied, "You are not worthy to utter the name of God or the Trinity, nor to lift up your hands to heaven, for your lips have been full of wickedness and your hands have wickedly touched filth" (106; p. 83 in this volume).

Thais redeems herself through her voluntary penance, and her worthiness is greater than that of the abbot and the other holy men: "When Paul said that the grace of the vision was due only to the merits of Saint Anthony, a heavenly voice said it was not by the merits of Anthony, but the merits of Thais, the sinful woman" (106; p. 84 in this volume). The monks are condemned for their arrogance in assuming that they brought this woman to salvation, and she is lauded for her repentance.

Her holiness is further illustrated when they open her cell door and she speaks about the extent of her penance: " 'As God is my witness, since I entered this cell, I have set all my sins before my eyes. Just as the breath never parts from the mouth or the nostrils, my sins never passed from my sight, but I have constantly beheld them and wept for them' " (107). In acknowledging her sin and serving her penance, Thais meekly accepts her fate without a word of contention. After Mary Magdalene, these "fallen women" barely have an audible voice at all. They view their penance as just and adhere to it, silently, but their silence does not render them powerless. Thais exercises a great deal of control over her own destiny by deciding to repent and acknowledging her failings. The author makes it clear that the only one responsible for Thais' salvation is herself. But prostitutes were only considered worthy examples if they repented. Carla Casagrande points out that many clerics would not even address women in that occupation, "The preacher, the moralist, and the teacher selected from reality, those categories of women which embodied, or had the potential to embody, the values he was proposing. Only women belonging to predetermined categories had the potential to be virtuous; the others were doubly doomed to social marginalization and a sinful life."[42] Mary Magdalene holds a unique position among her fellow sinners, resonating as a strident voice for women of ill repute, primarily because she was viewed as the ulti-

42 Carla Casagrande, "The Protected Woman" in Klapisch-Zuber, ed., *A History of Women in the West, vol. II: Silences of the Middle Ages*, pp. 74–5.

mate example of salvation. She occupies a special place in the canon of saints and her voice is used as an instrument of power, but it can be argued that the patristic authors who constructed her life from the fragments of historical material really wielded that instrument to appeal to a growing audience of women. Whatever the motivation of the biographers, repentant sinners served a definite purpose by providing clear examples of the possibilities of repentance and conversion and were probably used to encourage "lascivious" women to recognize the error of their ways and follow these role models.

Holy Transvestites

There are only five female saints in the entire *Gilte Legende* who fall into the category of transvestites, and three of them could also be counted among the sinful women. Throughout the medieval period prior to 1050, twenty-three stories about female transvestites were circulating in Europe.[43] Holy transvestitism is the adoption of the opposite gender, in dress and lifestyle, for a variety of reasons, whether it is to avoid marriage, to efface the female gender and thereby erase the sin considered natural to it, or simply as a means of survival. Saint Theodora, Saint Pelagia, and Saint Margaret Pelagia are all women who sin, taking refuge and penance for their sins dressed as men, living as monks in a monastery or as hermits. Saint Marina is raised as a boy in a monastery by her father, after the death of her mother, and encouraged by him to keep her gender a secret after his death. Their lives are included in this translation to show the different face of female sanctity; the one where a woman is sanctified because her brethren think she is a man. Unlike the two transvestites described in Leslie Donovan's *Women Saints' Lives in Old English Prose,* Eugenia and Euphrosyne, these women do not reveal their true gender, nor do they take any kind of defiant stand in defense of themselves or their sex. Except for Eugenia, listed in the *Gilte Legende* under the names of her male servants Protus and Hyacinthus, the sanctity of the transvestites rests solely on the fact that they say nothing when accused of fornication and accept an unjust punishment – quietly, patiently, and without protest. Both Eugenia and Euphrosyne are strong-minded women who have their own clear voice. During her examination before her father, the

43 Donovan, *Women Saints' Lives*, p. 67.

Roman judge, Eugenia "tore open her clothes and revealed her breasts to the famous Philippus."[44] This act of defiance is not mirrored in the accounts of the other holy transvestites in the *Gilte Legende*. In fact, Eugenia's sanctity is determined more by her open defiance and subsequent torture than by her three-year existence as a man.

For the other transvestites, sanctity is a direct result of their abandonment of their natural gender. In each case, except Saint Pelagia who lives as a hermit, these women are falsely accused of impregnating a local country girl, or in the case of Margaret Pelagia, a nun, and forced out of the monastery in disgrace to rear the child in abject poverty as a reminder of their sins. None of these women protest; in fact, very few of them speak at all, except Eugenia. The truth of their gender is not discovered until their death, after being admitted back into the confines of the monastery for serving out their penance so meekly. When their bodies are being prepared, their innocence is revealed and they are buried with great worship. Their gender is seen as a miracle when it is discovered, mainly because it went undetected before. The scribe changes the personal pronoun as the saint changes gender, from "she" to "he" and back to "she" to mirror the change in the reader's perception of the saint, as well as that of the monks living with her. Holy transvestitism implies that women can only be holy, or repent their sins of the flesh (except Saint Marina), by not being a woman. At her death, Saint Margaret (Pelagia) illustrates, in writing, how she lived as a man to repent for one sin, but died as a woman innocent of another:

> "I, of noble kindred, was called Margaret in the world. But because I wished to eschew the temptations of the world, I called myself Pelagian. I am a woman. I have not lied to deceive, because I have showed that I have the virtue of a man and I have had virtue from the crime that was put upon me, and I, innocent of that, have done the penance. But I pray you, for as much as men did not know I was a woman, let the holy sisters bury my body so the sight of my death may cleanse my life, and that the women will know I am a virgin who they judged as an adulterer" (126).

All of these legends highlight the meekness and patience of these saints, compared with their outspoken, but guiltless, counterparts. The important aspect of these legends is the knowledge and accep-

44 Donovan, *Women Saints' Lives*, p. 73.

tance of sin and then the decision to purge that sin by denying their gender. Marina, because she knows no sin, becomes the icon of purity and virginity: "Unlike these women, Marina begins monastic life as a pure innocent, virtually genderless. One may assume that she is not even conscious of her own virginity, hence that she is a true virgin, one not corrupted by even the knowledge of sexual things."[45] Marina is an anomaly in the tradition of saints' lives; she achieves sanctity and is revered, not for anything she does, but for everything she does not do and of which she is not conscious. She has no idea she will be venerated for accepting the false accusation and punishment, and in this way she becomes an apology for a monastic mistake. The abbot and her brethren must atone for their haste in believing one of their own capable of such a sin and for their mistreatment of an innocent. Brother Marinus neither denies nor admits his guilt; however, everyone jumps to that conclusion, which says more about the proclivities of medieval monks than about Marina's meekness or grace. So once their error is discovered, it is deemed a miracle, as Susanna Fein points out:

> By medieval misogynist thinking a woman who maintains her chastity by hiding her gender is already on the way to sainthood. If she endures the penitential vows and existence of a monk, compounded with an imposed penance designed for a man, she is doubly, even triply, proven. What marks her sainthood is not merely that she suffered innocently and grievously, but that she suffered as a man, being merely a woman. Her sainthood is thus figured in terms of a bigendering, which allows Marina to experience God in her lifetime as no man can.[46]

Marina is an example to other women and her fellow saints because she accepted her punishment, however unjust, in great humility and silence. The holy transvestites are an unusual group of women saints. Their lives are one example of how women "were able to capitalize on the handicaps and advantages afforded by the system of relations between the sexes"[47] precisely because they cease to be

45 Susanna Fein, "A Saint 'Geynest under Gore': Marina and the Love Lyrics of the Seventh Quire" in *Studies in the Harley Manuscript: The Scribes, Contents, and Scribal Contexts of British Library MS Harley 2253* (Kalamazoo, Mich.: Medieval Institute Publications, 2000) p. 363.

46 Fein, "A Saint 'Geynest under Gore'," pp. 363–4.

47 Christiane Klapisch-Zuber, ed., *A History of Women in the West, vol. II: Silences of the Middle Ages*, p. 161.

women. Their decision, while quietly executed, is powerful because they challenge the entire social structure of gender relations and place some women outside normal constraints lending to what Christiane Klapische-Zuber calls "the hidden power of women."[48]

These accounts from each of the four categories illustrate the power and influence female saints exerted in their legends and how these legends were held up as models for the women of the Middle Ages. From these stories arose massive cult followings for many of these saints; they were worshiped and venerated, to some extent out of fear and ignorance.[49] Klapisch-Zuber says, "In discussing historical change it is often easier for historians to agree about obstacles and impediments than about meaning. The facts are clear but their implications are not. The facts about the status of women can be read in different ways."[50] The legends of women saints provide some of these facts about the status of women, and they too can be read in many different ways, based on the context of the collection, the intended audience, and the identity of the author. However, one fact remains constant; women were a major part of hagiography and they left their mark upon it. According to Andrea Hopkins, "We think of the Middle Ages as being repressive, but it may surprise us to learn that women enjoyed more opportunities and suffered from fewer restrictions than in subsequent centuries until our own . . . But the weight of misogynist tradition and increasingly repressive legislation did not actually succeed in keeping women chained to the kitchen sink (so to speak) until well into what we think of as the modern era."[51]

Based on the text of the lives of women saints in the corpus of the *Gilte Legende*, it is evident that women were not as silent as some historians and scholars have suggested. These saints did not always serve their religion in silence and obedience. Their speech is very often an instrumental part of their sainthood; it defines them and places them above all others who are not willing to accept martyrdom or sacrifice for the Christian God. Defiant language is

48 Klapisch-Zuber, ed., *A History of Women in the West, vol. II: Silences of the Middle Ages*, p. 161.

49 Klapisch-Zuber, ed., *A History of Women in the West, vol. II: Silences of the Middle Ages*, p. 161.

50 Klapisch-Zuber, ed., *A History of Women in the West, vol. II: Silences of the Middle Ages*, p. 162.

51 Andrea Hopkins, *Most Wise and Valiant Ladies: Remarkable Lives of Women of the Middle Ages* (Oxford: Collins & Brown, 1997) p. 8.

what elevates these women from the records of the obscure where they would have been lost; the power of their speech is what makes their legends so extraordinary and interesting. At times, such as in the legends of the holy transvestites, the silence of these women speaks volumes about their faith and their endurance. Ecclesiastical male authors were the prime means by which these lives were transmitted, but the fact that they chose women as subjects suggests that not every woman was considered inferior and treacherous. While the author or scribe may have imposed his own agenda on the transmission of these lives, they established a precedent for allowing women to speak for themselves and their beliefs. This precedent did not fade during the course of the Middle Ages; in fact it flourished, despite accounts of docile women such as Elizabeth of Hungary. The lives of Christina, Dorothy, Margaret of Antioch, Paula, Elizabeth of Hungary, Mary Magdalene, Thais, Marina, Theodora, Pelagia, and Margaret Pelagia were widely read and popularly venerated throughout the Middle Ages in a number of vernaculars, including Middle English. The existence of these collections to this day speaks for their value and longevity. Women took up the pen after the example of these women and voiced their opposition to the Church Fathers who strove to keep them silent in their faith and their devotion. Writers like Christine de Pizan, Hildegard of Bingen, Marie de France, and Hrotswitha of Gandersheim are only a few women who left their mark on the literary world, combining their religious devotion and secular talent to establish a female literary tradition. The female saints of the *Gilte Legende* were held up as examples to medieval women and, for the most part, were vocal, authoritative, and eloquent, and it is best to let them speak for themselves.

Translator and Date of the *Gilte Legende*

Many of the *Gilte Legende* manuscripts refer to a Latin exemplar from which the story was translated, or as British Library MS Harley 630 says, “drawen into englissh bi worthi clerkes and doctours of Diuinite suengly after þe tenure of þe Latin” (drawn into English by worthy clerks and doctors of divinity faithfully after the fashion of the Latin). One manuscript, Bodleian Library MS Douce 372, says that the *Gilte Legende* is the English version for the Latin *Legenda Aurea*, “which was drawen out of Frensshe into Englisshe the yere of oure lorde, a MCCCC and xxxviij bi a synfulle wrecche” (Which was drawn out of French into English, the year of our Lord 1438 by a sinful wretch). The *Gilte Legende* is a product of translation and compilation, depending on the scribe who copied it. Harley MS 630 clearly says the material was translated directly from the Latin, while the Douce manuscript says it was translated from Latin to French and then into Middle English. This leads to a certain amount of variance in the contents of each manuscript as well as the text. These conflicting reports have been the starting point of many debates on the date and authorship, or rather translatorship, of the *Gilte Legende* as a whole.

At one time, Osbern Bokenham was advanced as a candidate for being the "sinful wretch" because he stated in his *Mappula Angliae* that he had written a collection of saints' lives compiled from the *Legenda Aurea* and "other famous legends."[52] Carl Horstmann put forth Bokenham's name and withdrew it because the *Gilte Legende* manuscripts known to him "contained none of the lives named."[53] Sister Mary Jeremy tentatively revived the argument when new manuscripts, which did contain some of these lives, came to light. Richard Hamer has since called her theory into question and has advanced one of his own based on the passage at the end of *Saint Alban* which refers to the author of *Alban* as being "sinful" and "wretched." However, this section of *Alban* is a direct translation of William's *Vita,* one of the Latin sources used in the compilation of the *Life of Saint Alban and Amphibalus*. Hamer also suggests that the *Gilte Legende* collection was compiled and possibly translated at Saint Alban's monastery.[54] This placement of the collection shows how widely disseminated the text was and how certain lives were added or omitted depending on the location of the manuscript at the time of production. The translator may have produced the manuscript himself, or worked closely with the scribe who compiled it, resulting in the many variations in content in the different manuscripts. There have been many discussions over the years as to the history and provenance of the *Gilte Legende*, but the most important aspect of this debate is how widely it was circulated and who owned copies of it. Considering the date in the Douce manuscript, dating the *Gilte Legende* collection to the early-fifteenth or late-fourteenth century seems the most plausible. This collection of saints' lives was circulated at a time when the world was at war; the countries of Europe

52 Richard Hamer, *Three Lives from the "Gilte Legende" edited from MS BL Egerton 876* (Heidelberg: Universitätsverlag Carl Winter, 1978) p. 17.

53 Carl Horstmann, quoted in Hamer, *Three Lives from the "Gilte Legende"*, p. 6.

54 Establishing the provenance of Harley MS 630 is the focus of my article in the *Journal of the Early Book Society*, vol. 3, "British Library MS Harley 630: Saint Alban's and Lydgate" (New York: Pace University Press, 2000) pp. 36–58.

were fighting among themselves and within their own borders. The Wars of the Roses were at their height and women, such as Elizabeth Woodville, wife of the Yorkist king Edward IV, were exercising a great deal of power and wielding their influence. It is in this climate of struggle and change that the Middle English version of these legends was translated, compiled, and disseminated, perhaps as a reminder of the role of religion, faith, and defiance in the face of tyranny and oppression.

Sources for the Lives of Female Saints

The majority of the saints' lives in the *Gilte Legende* are taken from Jacobus de Voragine's *Legenda Aurea.* Jacobus, in turn, took his legends from a variety of sources, sometimes using the works of Church Fathers, such as Saint Ambrose and Saint Jerome. Jacobus left a list of his major works, six in total, in his *Chronicle of Genoa*, probably written between 1295 and 1297.[55] These works include the *Chronicle* itself, the *Legenda Aurea*, a *Marialis*, and three volumes of sermons.[56] Jacobus often lists the source for each legend in the etymology before each life. These etymologies are a unique feature of Jacobus' *Legenda Aurea* and are not included in the *Gilte Legende*, showing the extent to which a particular scribe could alter and manipulate a text depending on his own agenda. Jacobus uses the popular saints of the liturgical calendar for his collection, using the most up-to-date lives of the most recent saints. Due to the overriding desire for current material, many of the legends vary in style, length, and content; for example, in *Saint Elizabeth*, Jacobus may have turned to the most readily available material, the official documentation of her canonization, to write her legend.[57] However, he acknowledges his three main sources as the *Ecclesiastical History* of Eusebius, the *Tripartite History* of Cassiodorus, and the *Scholastic History* of Peter Comestor.[58] Jacobus also says that he adds many things of his own.

Hamer points out that "a substantial proportion of the *Legenda Aurea* was closely derived from works by two Dominicans, Jean de Mailly's *Summary of the Deeds and Miracles of Saints* (a lengthy work, despite its title) and Bartholomew of Trent's *Afterword on the*

55 Richard Hamer, introduction to *The Golden Legend: Selections*, by Jacobus de Voragine, ed. by Christopher Stace (Harmondsworth: Penguin Books, 1998) p. x.

56 Hamer, Introduction to *The Golden Legend*, p. x.

57 Hamer, Introduction to *The Golden Legend*, p. xii.

58 Hamer, Introduction to *The Golden Legend*, p. xii.

Deeds of the Saints."[59] In cases where Jacobus turns to a single life for his source material, he is careful to say so, as in the life of Paula. However, Jacobus is not always explicit about the source for individual legends and in some cases says nothing at all. Because of this, many medieval scribes were given a certain amount of freedom to interpret and revise the legends they were translating as they saw fit. The absence of traceable sources for these legends makes their Middle English form a valuable record of the mindset and attitudes directed toward a medieval female audience, especially since many of the saints did not exist, at least not in the miraculous capacity ascribed to them. Jacobus enhanced and embellished the legends in his collection, as did the scribes after him who added material for a specific purpose, in many cases, as propaganda for their house or order, or to suit a particular agenda. The fictitious nature of the saints' legends, including eight of those included in this edition, should not negate their value for a medieval audience. Carolyne Larrington explains that the medieval definition of "history" needs to be considered when reading these accounts: "the modern reader needs to revise her own definition of history as 'fact' in order to interpret them."[60] A majority of saints' legends may deal in fiction by the modern definition, but to the medieval reader they were accepted as historical accounts, however fantastic.[61]

I would like to express my gratitude to the following people for their invaluable contribution to my research: Julia Boffey, Diane Bolton, Ian Doyle, Martha Driver, A. S. G. Edwards, Derek Pearsall, Pam Robinson, and John Flood. I would like to thank Richard Hamer and Vida Russell for their guidance, support and assistance; Mark Chambers, Angie Gleason, and Aisling Hayden for their tireless efforts; and Owen Delaney for going through the Latin passage at the end of *Saint Dorothy* and providing the translation.

I would also like to thank my colleagues at Mary Washington College, Georgetown University, and George Mason University for their support, suggestions, and encouragement; they include, but are

[59] Hamer, Introduction to *The Golden Legend*, p. xiii.

[60] Carolyne Larrington, *Women and Writing in Medieval Europe* (London: Routledge, 1995) p. 1.

[61] Jane Tibbetts Schulenburg examines the validity of saints' lives as historical record in her article "Saints' Lives as a Source" and in her study on female sanctity, *Forgetful of Their Sex: Female Sanctity and Society ca. 500–1100* (Chicago: University of Chicago Press, 1998).

not limited to Penn Szittya, Sarah McNamer, Bill Kemp, and Teresa Kennedy. I also owe many thanks to Jane Chance and Caroline Palmer for their patience and guidance, and to Terry Munisteri for proofreading this manuscript.

I owe an enormous debt of gratitude to John Scattergood for his direction, guidance, support, and patience during the course of this work. I also owe an immeasurable debt to my mother, Nina Zerkich, who made this possible, and to Rikk Mulligan for everything. Finally, I would like to thank the manuscript department at Trinity College, Dublin, the British Library, and the Bodleian Library, Oxford, for their assistance in compiling this edition.

Note to the Translations

All the translations in this work are drawn from my transcriptions of British Library MS Harley 630 and Trinity College, Dublin Library MS 319 that were part of my D.Phil dissertation at Trinity College, Dublin. *Dorothy* and *Mary Magdalene* are taken from TCD MS 319, the rest from Harley MS 630. I have tried to preserve the tone and style of the Middle English author while making the text accessible and enjoyable for a modern audience. At times, the meaning has been obscured by the original translation from Latin into Middle English, and I have tried to clarify it as much as possible. When necessary, I have included footnotes to further explain or interpret the original text.

Saint Christina

Saint Christina of Tyre, whose life is part of the *Legenda Aurea* and the later Middle English *Gilte Legende*, did not exist. She is the eastern counterpart of Saint Christina of Bolsena; their legends are almost identical, as is their feast day, July 24.[1] The legends diverge when Christina of Tyre is martyred with arrows, while Christina of Bolsena survives the arrows and is martyred by an axe blow to the head. Both saints are represented in iconography with a millstone around their neck, a reminder of the attempt made to drown them in the ocean. The description of Christina's grave at the end of the legend indicates that Jacobus was familiar with the saint's association with Bolsena, while the Middle English scribe lists her burial place as "a castle called Buffe, in between Orbenice, Viterbe and Tyre that is beside the castle that was later destroyed." There is no source given for this most gruesome of female saints' lives; however, in the *Legenda Aurea*, Jacobus de Voragine provides an etymology for the saint's name: "Saint Christina's name suggests *chrismate uncta*, anointed with chrism. She had the balm of good odour in her relationships with others and the oil of devotion in her mind and benediction in her speech."[2] The Middle English scribe omits the etymology, but retains all the elements of her speech within the legend.

Christina, who was martyred during the reign of Diocletian in AD 247, is, like most early Christian saints, a woman of noble birth who converts in defiance of her family. Her legend falls into the category of "ryght hooly virgynes" because she defends her body from the unwanted sexual advances of two different judges after refusing to submit to the pagan doctrine of her father. She is violently tortured and executed, but her voice echoes through the centuries, speaking out, even after her tongue is removed, when many of her brethren are

1 Gaston Duchet-Suchaux and Michel Pastoureau, *The Bible and the Saints* (New York: Flammarion, 1994) p. 88.

2 William Granger Ryan, *The Golden Legend: Readings on the Saints* (Princeton: Princeton University Press, 1993) vol. 1, p. 385.

silent in their devotion and meek in their martyrdom. The life of Saint Christina translated here is from my transcription of Harley MS 630.

The Life of Saint Christina

Christina was born of noble kindred from Tyre, in Italy and her father put her in a tower with seven handmaidens and idols of gold and silver. Because she was very beautiful, many desired to take her as their wife, but her father would grant her to no one. Instead, he wished she would stay and worship their gods. But she, who was taught by the Holy Ghost, dreaded sacrificing to idols and hid the incense with which the sacrifice was given in a window alcove.

In time, when her father came to visit her, her servants told him, "Your daughter, that is our lady, will not perform sacrifice to our gods, and she says she is a Christian." Her father flattered her and cajoled her to make her do sacrifice, but she replied, "Praise belongs to me because I offer sacrifice to the God of Heaven and not to inanimate gods." Her father answered, "My daughter, do not offer sacrifice to one god above, lest the other gods become angry with you." She responded, "You have spoken wisely, you who are unknowing, for I offer to God the Father, to God the Son, to God the Holy Ghost; three people and one God." Her father said, "If you worship three gods, why do you not worship others as well?" She answered, "Because these three that I worship is one Godhead."

Her father left her there and Christina took all his idols, broke them, and gave the gold and silver to the poor. After that, her father came back to worship his gods, but he did not find them, and the servants told him what Christina had done. Her father commanded her to be stripped and beaten by twelve men until they were weary. Christina said to her father, "Oh thou without worship or shame, and abominable to God, see you not how they have fallen? Pray to your gods that give them virtue and strength." He ordered her to be chained fast and put in prison.

When Christina's mother heard what had happened, she tore her clothes, ran to the prison, and fell down at the feet of her daughter, crying, "Ah, daughter Christina, the light of my eye, have pity on me." Christina replied, "Why do you call me your daughter? Do you not know well that I have the name of my God?" When she could not persuade her, Christina's mother returned to her husband and told him Christina's answer. Her father had her brought before him for judgment.

He said to her, "Sacrifice to our gods or else you shall suffer diverse torments and you shall no more be called my daughter." Christina replied, "Now you have done me a great grace since I shall no longer be called the devil's daughter, for he that is born of the devil is the devil, and you are the father of that same evil."

He commanded her tender flesh to be torn with hooks and her limbs torn apart. Christina took a handful of her flesh and threw it at her father, saying, "Hold, you tyrant, and eat your flesh that you have begotten." Then her father set her on a wheel with fire and oil under it, but such a flame erupted that it killed 1,500 men. Her father attributed all this to magic, ordered that she be thrown in prison again, and commanded that, as soon as it was night, they should bind a great stone around her neck and cast her into the sea.

When she was tossed into the sea, the angels took hold of her and Jesus Christ descended to her, baptizing her in the sea, saying, "I baptize you in the name of God, my Father, and in my name, Jesus Christ, his Son, and of the Holy Ghost." He commended her to Saint Michael the Archangel who brought her to land. When her father heard this, he struck himself on the forehead saying, "By what witchcraft do you do such magic in the sea?" She replied, "You cursed wretch, I have this power from Jesus Christ."

That same night, Urban, her father, was found dead. After him came a corrupt judge called Zienius,[3] who ordered a large vessel of iron, full of pitch, oil, and tar. When it was burning, he had Christina cast into the middle and made four men move the vessel about so that she would be completely washed in it. Christina praised Jesus Christ, by whom she had been newly christened, as he rocked her like a child in a cradle.

The judge prepared to behead her and had her led naked through the city into the temple of Apollo. There she commanded the idol to fall, and the statue fell, crumbling into powder. When the judge heard this, he died of fear. He was succeeded by Julian, who had a furnace stoked and Christina cast into it. She was there five days singing with angels and emerged from it unharmed. When Julian heard this, he believed it was all done through enchantment and released two adders, two serpents, and two asps on her. But these serpents licked her feet; the two asps hung at her breasts and did not harm her; and

3 "Elius" in Ryan, *The Golden Legend*, vol. 1, p. 387.

the adders wound themselves about her neck and licked her nose. Julian said to his magician, “Are you not cunning enough to move these serpents?” But as soon as he stirred them, they made straight for him and killed him. Christina ordered the serpents into desert places, and she raised the dead man from death to life.

Julian then commanded that her breasts be cut off, and when they were, milk flowed out of them instead of blood. After that, he made them cut out her tongue, but she never lost her power of speech; instead she took the dismembered piece of her tongue, threw it in the judge’s face, and struck out both his eyes with it. Julian was angered and had two arrows shot at her heart and one toward her side. When the arrows struck her, she yielded up her spirit to our Lord about the year of our Lord 247, under Diocletian.[4] The holy body rested in a castle called Buffe, in between Orbenice, Viterbe, and Tyre – that is, beside the castle that was later destroyed.[5] Here ends the life of Saint Christina.

4 Diocletian, Roman emperor c. AD 245–313.

5 “Her body rests near a fortified place called Bolsena between Orvieto and Viterbo; the tower which was once near that town has been completely demolished” (Ryan, *The Golden Legend*, vol. 1, p. 387). Ryan has “tower” but points out that Graesse suggested “tyrus” (tyro) instead of “turris” (tower). The Middle English scribe used “castle.”

Saint Dorothy

The legend of Saint Dorothy is not part of the *Gilte Legende* corpus, nor does she appear in the *Legenda Aurea.* My translation is from the fragment found in Trinity College, Dublin Library MS 319 (TCD MS 319), that contains a section of the *Gilte Legende* bound with two legends, *Dorothy* and *Catherine* that were probably circulated on their own. There is no known source for this version of *Dorothy*, though the story is the same as that found in Osbern Bokenham's *Legendys of Hooly Wummen* and there are many parallels between the texts. The life may have been a popular devotional circulated on its own and given to Bokenham for inclusion in his collection of female saints' lives. It is possible that the version of *Dorothy* translated here is either a prose copy of Bokenham's *Dorothy* or his source.[1] Bokenham lists the names of Dorothy's sisters as Trystem and Kalystem. The version of *Dorothy* found in the Middle English collection the *Additional Lives,* described by Richard Hamer and Vida Russell as "Dorothy 1," gives the names Cristyne and Calistyne.[2] The second version in their edition, a close translation of the original Latin and an earlier version than that of the *Additional Lives*, is listed as "Dorothy 2," and names them Cristem and Calistem.[3] Only the third version found in TCD MS 319 identifies them as Trystem and Calystem. Another important correlation can be made when Theophilus, the doctor of law converted by Dorothy, is introduced. Bokenham describes him as "Oon Theophyl preyid hyr schornfully,/ Whych prothonotarye was of that kingdam (One Theophilus begged her scornfully, who was the protonotary of that kingdom)."[4] One version describes him as "Theophilus, the

1 I will only touch on the major points of this theory here; the bulk of these examples and ideas were the focus of the conference paper I delivered at the International Congress of Medieval Studies at the University of Western Michigan in Kalamazoo, May 2000.

2 Richard Hamer and Vida Russell, *Supplementary Lives in Some Manuscripts of the "Gilte Legende"* Early English Text Society, original series 315 (Oxford: Oxford University Press, 2000).

3 Hamer and Russell, *Supplementary Lives.*

4 Osbern Bokenham, *Legendys of Hooly Wummen*, ed. by Mary Serjeantson, Early

scribe of the realm."[5] Another describes him as "Theophilus the great notary of the realm."[6] The version closest to Bokenham's is the one in TCD MS 319, which uses the same words to describe this future martyr: "Oone Theophilus, whyche was the prothonotary chyef of that region" (One Theophilus, who was protonotary chief of that region). The details surrounding the execution and disposal of Theophilus' body, combined with these pieces of evidence, give a more definite idea of which came first, the poetry or the prose. In Bokenham, Theophilus is martyred and "For on many smal pecys hys body he hew/ And to bestys & fowlys þe gobettys he threw" (For in many small pieces his body was hewn and to beasts and birds the gobbets he threw).[7] Neither of the other two versions of *Dorothy* use graphic language to illustrate this particularly nasty fate. One states "at last he was cut al to smale pecis and his flesshe cast to bestes and briddys to be devoured" (at last he was cut to small pieces and his flesh cast to beasts and birds to be devoured).[8] The other is equally uninteresting and rather mundane: "Att the last he was cutt all in smalle peces and comavnded to be caste to beastis and to byrdes for to be devoured" (At last he was cut into small pieces and ordered to be cast to beasts and birds to be devoured).[9] However, the version of *Dorothy* in TCD MS 319 goes into a great deal of detail, expanding on his torment and the cruelty of his executioners: "And at the last he commaunded hym to be all tohewen into small gobettes, as who choppeth flesshe to the pot, and tho pieces of hys flesshe to be cast to bestes and to byrdes, and so malycyously and tyrauntly to be devoured" (And at last he commanded that he be hewn into small gobbets, like those who chop flesh for the pot, and those pieces of his flesh thrown to beasts and birds to be tyrantly devoured). The use of the words "gobettes" and "hew" or "hewn" connects these two texts and separates them from the other extant versions of *Dorothy*. The textual comparison shows that Bokenham most likely used the same source as the version extant as a fragment in TCD MS 319. The rhyme scheme of Bokenham's poetry does not exist in the prose version, indicating that Bokenham either had the fragment or the originally complete version of *Dorothy* and *Catherine* in TCD MS

English Text Society, original series 206 (Oxford: Oxford University Press, 1938) lines 4891–2.

5 Hamer and Russell, *Supplementary Lives*, line 89.

6 Hamer and Russell, *Supplementary Lives*, lines 83–4.

7 Bokenham, *Legendys of Hooly Wummen*, lines 4965–6.

8 Hamer and Russell, *Supplementary Lives*, lines 139–40.

9 Hamer and Russell, *Supplementary Lives*, lines 129–30.

319, along with whatever else it may have contained, as he compiled his *Legendys* for various female patrons. Perhaps this fragment belonged to one of those women who asked Bokenham to include this version of *Dorothy* in his compilation. The relationship with Bokenham's text shows that while the legend of Dorothy is not included in the majority of hagiographical collections, of which the *Gilte Legende* is only one, it was popular enough to establish a cult in her honor and a substantial following. Christine de Pizan includes Dorothy among the saints she describes in *The Book of the City of Ladies* for being constant during her martyrdom.[10] There are almost no historical details about Dorothy's life and no source is ever given for her legend. The material surrounding the invention of her cult and the properties of her martyrdom is sketchy at best and does not provide a definitive marker pointing to a clear order of transmission. Hamer points out that Dorothy is believed to have been martyred c. 300: "Two versions of her life place her either in Caesarea under the governor Fabricius during the persecutions of Diocletian, or in Alexandria under Maximian. The manuscripts of Dorothy's life in English known to us contain the Caesarea story."[11]

Dorothy, like Christina, is of noble birth and chooses a gruesome death rather than marriage to a local prefect. She voices her defiance but is not quite as evocative as Christina, dwelling more on her relationship with Christ as His spouse. Her speech is described as meek and faithful, but she does not back down in the face of violent and prolonged torture. Her cult grew in popularity around the fifteenth century and was focused primarily in Germany and Italy.[12] She is pictured in art and sculpture with a basket of roses and apples or a crown of roses and the Christ Child.[13]

The Life of Saint Dorothy

This glorious virgin and martyr Dorothy, whose father's name was Dorotheus and whose mother's name was Theodora, came from the noble progeny of the most famous and worthiest senators of Rome. In her day, the grievous persecution of Christian people everywhere

10 Christine de Pizan, *The Book of the City of Ladies*, trans. by Earl Jeffrey Richards (New York: Persea Books, 1998) III.9.3, p. 233.

11 Hamer and Russell, *Supplementary Lives*, p. 225.

12 Gaston Duchet-Suchaux and Michel Pastoureau, *The Bible and the Saints* (New York: Flammarion, 1994) p. 127.

13 Duchet-Suchaux and Pastoureau, *The Bible and the Saints*, p. 128.

grew greatly, causing the blessed Dorotheus, father of this holy virgin, who hated and despised the cursed and abominable necromancy of the Romans, to forsake the country and fellowship of the loathsome Romans, including all his possessions of castles, houses, lands, rents, and vineyards with all other riches. He passed over the sea with his good wife, Theodora, and his two daughters whose names were Trystem and Calystem. They came to the region of Cappadocia, entered into a fair city of that region called Ceasarea, and lived there, wherein a gracious daughter was begotten, and of whose life now, with the grace of God, we propose to speak.

When this holy virgin was born, following the holy custom of the Christian religion, she was christened in secret by the holy bishop Saint Apollinarus, who compounded her father's name with her mother's and named the child Dorothea. Soon after, when nature had advanced this gracious and holy virgin with more maturity, though she was still a tender age, she was so replenished with the diversity of virtues of the Holy Ghost in all ways, in body as in soul, and so sufficiently taught in gracious virtuousness that everyone saw how nature had so excellently advanced her with singular beauty. The fame of her beauty, along with her other singular virtues, overshadowed all the maidens of that region.

The enemy of all mankind, the devil in hell, envied this virtuous bounty so much that he could not abide any creature to profit who intended to grow in virtuous living, especially that excellent virtue of angelic chastity which he knew well that this young, chosen virgin aspired to at such an innocent age, and whose virtuous fame clearly shone throughout that region. So he stirred, moved, and greatly excited one of his lecherous disciples, Fabricius by name, who held the office of prefect, and by whom passed all the judgments of that region.

This wretched, blind, lecherous tyrant, so greatly moved and stirred with fleshly concupiscence, was so sorely oppressed by his unlawful desire for this glorious virgin that his blind nature could not stand it. Wherefore in all haste, under the guise of his office, he sent for her and opened to this chosen virgin the sinful treasure of his abominable desires, promising her such a bounty of treasure with plenty of other worldly goods that he thought would please her youth, without any thought to her virtues, and also promising to wed her lawfully after the custom of the region.

This chaste, sweet, and gracious virgin – when she heard his unclean and blind desires, his rich promises of his earthly treasures, sayings, and behests – maidenly, holily, and with loathing indignation, utterly despised him as she would have done clay or any other earthly corruption. She openly declared herself and boldly in her virginal language said and acknowledged by her answer that she was married to her love and faith in spiritual matrimony as a true wife to our Savior, Jesus Christ.

When this blind and lecherous tyrant heard this holy virgin's answer, being glad that under the guise of the office of his prefecture he might execute the malicious vengeance conceived in his unclean heart, he suddenly became so angry in his furious tyranny that in all haste possible he commanded his torturers, without more language or tarrying, to cast that glorious virgin into a brass tun full of fervently boiling hot oil. But that blessed and loving lord, Jesus Christ, who comforts all his lovers in their greatest need and is the chief refuge for all his lovers in all manner of tribulation, quickly showed his mighty hand of loving and comfortable help to this gracious virgin Dorothy so that she felt nothing but unfettered bliss, without any pain from that torment. Wherefore she greatly rejoiced, thanking her spouse Jesus so lovingly, as though she had been anointed or bathed in the most precious and redolent balm on earth. Soon after this miracle was seen, many of the pagans who were present watching her painful torment, saw this great miracle of this chosen virgin and privately decided within themselves to be baptized in all possible haste, and many were secretly converted.

When this blind tyrant Fabricius saw this great miracle, he trusted and wholly believed that it had been done by some form of magic, otherwise known as necromancy. He quickly ordered this blessed virgin to be enclosed in a dark prison for nine days, meatless and drinkless without any manner of food or sustenance. But this blessed virgin in all the time of her imprisonment was nourished and fed by blessed angels with heavenly food. When she was brought forth before this cursed judge and he saw her beauty had increased manifold so that she was much more fair than ever she was before, and all the people who saw her beauty marveled greatly at how so tender a virgin who was kept so long without any food might appear so beautiful, this tyrant blinded by malice said to her, "Truly, unless you worship my gods immediately, you shall not escape the punishment of this sharp bed of iron which is full of sharp metal spikes."

This holy Dorothy answered meekly, "I worship God and no devils, for your gods that you worship are nothing else but devils." Then suddenly this blessed virgin fell down prostrate to the ground, lifting up her eyes to heaven, praying to Almighty God in his eternal goodness to show them how he is mighty and that there is no other God but he alone.

In the meantime, while this blessed virgin was in devout prayer to Almighty God, this tyrant Fabricius had a great pillar erected upon which he had set the chief object of his idolatry, which he worshiped most with his pagan ways as his god. Immediately God sent a great multitude of angels from heaven and with great hasty vengeance threw this cursed and loathsome monument to the ground with the pillar that it stood on so that no part of the pillar could be found. Suddenly, therewith, the voices of devils were heard crying in the air, "Oh Dorothy, why do you consume us and drive us from our possessions and dwelling places? You live too long on this earth." Immediately, a thousand pagans openly and faithfully converted to the Christian faith and then entered the kingdom of heaven by the victorious death of martyrdom.

Dorothy was quickly hanged upon a gibbet or gallows with her feet upward and her head downward, and with hooks of iron her fair and tender body was completely rent and torn; with small rods they beat her and with great whips sorely wounded her. After all these diverse torments were inflicted on her, burning brands were put to her maidenly breasts until they were consumed and burned away. Thus she was left half dead and sent to a bleak prison until the next day.

The next day when she was brought forth, this tyrant who was her judge saw clearly that there was no wound or token of her former torments on any part of her beautiful body, so much so that he marveled greatly. He said to her, "Oh sweet and beautiful virgin, do you remember any part of our conversation, for you have been somewhat chastised for your inordinate rebellion." He sent her two sisters, Trystem and Calystem – who had, for dread of temporal death, forsaken Christ and turned to the pagan law – to her so that, by her two sisters, if they could bring it about, this blessed virgin Dorothy would forsake Christ and turn again to pagan law as they had.

But blessed Dorothy spoke meekly and faithfully to her sisters, so blessedly and so heavenly that she took from them the blindness of their hearts at that time and converted them both again to the Christian faith. As this tyrant Fabricius heard this, he commanded that both these sisters be bound together, back to back, and be cast into a great fire to be burned, and so they were.

He said to Dorothy, "How long will you deceive us in this way with your enchantments and witchcraft, prolonging your life in such a manner? Either do sacrifice as you owe to our gods so that you may live, or else your head shall be struck off." This holy virgin answered with glad cheer and said, "Whatever pains you can think of, I am ready to suffer for the love of my lord and Savior Jesus Christ, my chosen spouse, in whose garden, so plenteously full of all manner of delights, I have gathered roses with apples, where I shall joy with him world without end."

When this tyrant, blinded in malice, heard how joyfully she answered, growing angry and wrathful, with malice fretting him sorely by the heart, in his cursed way grimacing and frowning, he commanded with a high, angry voice that her fair visage, singularly replenished with beauty, should be beaten with staves and blows so that no impression of her fair face might be known. It was done until her tormentors grew so weary that they could no longer sustain it. She was sent again to prison to be kept there until the next day.

The next day, when this glorious virgin Dorothy was brought forth before this tyrant, her judge, amazingly no sign of injury appeared on her maidenly body or face, because the night before she was healed and cured by our Savior Jesus Christ. When this tyrant saw this miracle, which he could not understand for lack of faith, he gave sentence of judgment that her head should be stricken off. Quickly she was led outside the walls of the city toward her judgment, where one Theophilus,[14] who was the protonotary of that region and the most solemn doctor of law in that whole country, saw this glorious virgin being led toward her death and spoke to her in a scorning manner. Mockingly, he prayed her to send him some roses from her spouse's garden, as he had heard her say before her cursed judge at the time of her passion, and in this way he often scornfully begged her. This blessed virgin, full of faith, immediately promised to send him what he desired, notwithstanding that at the time he desired this it was icy cold because it was the winter season, when all the earth is barren.

When this glorious virgin came to the place where her head should be struck off, she prayed to Our Lord for all of those who, in honor and worship of Almighty God, did any kind of thing in remembrance of her passion, that it might be the cause of their salvation – especially from the worldly shame of grievous poverty, also that they be delivered from shameful slander and loss of their name. She also prayed that they might have grace before they depart from this life, to have true contrition and have true remission from all their sins. She

14 Theophilus, the solemn doctor of law and, later, Christian martyr and saint.

prayed for all women who, with devotion in her name, pray or call for help, especially in the time of childbirth, so that they may have relief and aid from their sorrows and ailments. Finally, she prayed that in whatever house a book of her passion or an image of her was kept in remembrance, it might be preserved from all manner of peril from fire, and that no manner of lightning hurt it.

Directly after this prayer a voice was heard from heaven above, "Come on, my well beloved. Come on, my spouse. You have been granted in heaven all your petitions and requests, and also those you pray for shall be saved." Then she bowed down her head to the stroke of the executioner.

Suddenly there appeared an exceedingly fair child clothed in purple, with bare legs and feet, with curled hair, whose garment was powdered with stars, bearing a little basket in his hand with three roses and as many apples. He offered them to this blessed virgin Dorothy, and this glorious virgin said, "I beseech you, my lord, bear these roses and apples to the Doctor Theophilus." As this was said, she bowed her head and suffered the stroke of the sword, and she passed to God. On February 8 she suffered her martyrdom by the judge Fabricius, under the emperors of Rome, Diocletian, and Maximilian, the year of Christ's Incarnation 248.

At this time, mighty Theophilus, doctor of their law, stood in the judge's palace when this fair child, mentioned before, came to him, took him aside, and gave him this little basket with roses and apples, saying, "These roses with apples my sister sent from the delicious Garden of Paradise of her spouse Jesus." Then this fair child disappeared so suddenly that no creature could guess where he had gone. Immediately this famous doctor Theophilus broke out into a high, loud voice of loving and praising, glorifying and greatly magnifying Jesus Christ, the great God of the virgin Dorothy, who, in the month of February, in such great cold and frost which at that time had frozen the earth, when neither field nor orchard in nature knows greenness, nor bough can bear leaves [sent him these gifts]. "Such roses and apples this mighty lord Jesus graciously sends to whom he will; whose mighty, gracious, and glorious name must ever be blessed, world without end. Amen." Because of his testimony and affirmation, and by his preaching, the whole city was converted to the faith of our Savior, was baptized and received into Christendom.

When this cursed tyrant and judge Fabricius saw that this great doctor Theophilus had converted the people and the whole city, he commanded that Theophilus be tormented with many kinds of torture, many more than Dorothy was tormented with. At last, he commanded that Theophilus be hewn into small gobbets, like those chopped up for the pot, and that those pieces of his flesh be cast to the beasts and birds and so maliciously and tyrannical devoured.

But this gracious doctor Theophilus had first received the sacrament of baptism and was also blessed with the precious sacrament of Christ's glorious flesh and blood. So, by holy martyrdom, full of faith, he followed that blessed and glorious virgin Dorothy and exchanged this mortal life and passed to our Savior Jesus Christ, who glorifies his lovers and saints. Our Savior Jesus is glorified in them that with the father and the Holy Ghost, together and coeternally, live and reign as God, into the world of worlds. Amen.

Antiphon:[15] "In whatever house the name or image taken from the blessed virgin martyr Dorothy (may be found) nothing shall be born prematurely. That house should feel no dangers of fire or theft. Nor would anyone suffer both evil pain and death. You will warn us about perjury against nature and the holy bread, through Jesus Christ, our Lord.

"The pious virgin Dorothy, potent in miracles, by the stains of our sins brought us into our peace and passed her entire life defending us against dangers. Pray for us unworthy, O martyr of Christ, who conquered the worldly flesh of the devil. Pray for us, blessed Dorothy, so we may be made worthy according to Christ. Let us pray. [I pray] all powerful and most gentle God, in whose name the glorious virgin and martyr Dorothy surpassed many kinds of torture, let us humbly pray that, by her intervention, we may be led, according to our necessity, through many dangers to her, and that, by your trials, we may realize you as our [blessed] helper, through Jesus Christ, our Lord, your Son, who lives and reigns with you for all eternity."

15 The Latin *antiphona* is complete, though space has been left at the bottom of the leaf. The first fragment of TCD MS 319 ends after *Dorothy* and the *Gilte Legende* fragment begins. This is an approximate translation. Many thanks to Owen Delaney at Trinity College, Dublin who struggled through the transcription of this damaged section of the manuscript with me and came up with the above translation.

Saint Margaret of Antioch

Jacobus says the legend of Saint Margaret was written by "Theotimus, a learned man" but gives no other clue to his identity. He also quotes a "certain saint," which, according to Ryan, may be a reference to Ambrose who wrote the lives of virgin saints. At the same time Jacobus indicates the story may be fictitious, stating that the legend "about the beast swallowing the maiden and bursting asunder is considered apocryphal and not to be taken seriously."[1] However, Jacobus and the *Gilte Legende* scribe both refer to this version of her life, so it must have been a popular rendition that people would have recognized. Another version of the legend claims that, when the dragon swallowed her, she was able to cut open his belly with a small crucifix she carried with her and escape.[2] One of the unique attributes of her legend is the physicality of her defiance; Juliana is the only other saint who thrashes a demon. Not only is Margaret vocal and outspoken; she literally takes the devil by the horns (or in this case, the hair), throws him to the ground, and stomps on his neck until he tells her the truth about his pursuit of Christian souls. She demands answers to her questions, and the devil makes a point of saying how embarrassing it is to be vanquished by a mere slip of a girl before he responds, citing Old Testament apocrypha and the Book of Isaiah. Jacobus does not mention Lucifer's fall from grace, so this is an addition by the Middle English scribe, but it highlights the deep, despicable nature of the devil and the enduring battle between Satan and God, in which Margaret is a faithful soldier of Christ. It also exemplifies the importance of a female saint in facing and destroying evil in its purest form; it is her strength of will and devotion that allows her to triumph, and though she is a women, she is given the power, through her speech and actions, to defeat her foe.

1 William Granger Ryan, *The Golden Legend: Readings on the Saints* (Princeton: Princeton University Press, 1993) vol. 1, p. 369.

2 Gaston Duchet-Suchaux and Michel Pastoureau, *The Bible and the Saints* (New York: Flammarion, 1994) p. 228.

The Life of Saint Margaret of Antioch

Saint Margaret, daughter of Theodosius, a pagan patriarch, was born in the city of Antioch and delivered to a nurse. When she grew to the perfect age[3] she was baptized as a Christian, and because of this her father hated her greatly.

One day when she was fifteen years old, she was tending her nurse's sheep with other maidens when the provost Olybrius passed nearby. He considered the beauty of this virgin and was seized by love for her. Moved, he quickly sent messengers to the maidens, saying to them, "Go and take that maiden. If she is a free born woman, I will take her as my wife; but if she is a slave, I shall make her my concubine."[4]

When she was presented to him, he asked her name and inquired about her family and her religion. She answered that her name was Margaret, she came from a noble family, and was Christian. The provost addressed her: "The first two attributes fit you well because you are amicable, noble, and have proven that you are a fair pearl.[5] But the third attribute does not apply; such a fair and noble maid should not worship a god who was crucified." She replied, "Do you know that God was crucified?" He said, "Yes, through the books of Christian men." She retorted, "What a shame it is for you when you read in those books about the might and glory of him but do not believe in the former and renege the latter." She affirmed that Christ had been crucified of His own will for the redemption of mankind.

The provost commanded that she be locked in prison. The following day he called her before him and said, "You empty and vain maid, have pity for your beauty and worship our gods." She responded, "I worship God for whom the earth trembles, whom the sea dreads, and the wind and all creatures obey." The provost said, "If

3 Ryan translates this as "age of reason" (*The Golden Legend*, vol. 1, p. 368) that implies puberty. For further information on the "perfect age" see Kim Phillips, "Maidenhood as the Perfect Age of Woman's Life" in *Young Medieval Women*, ed. Katherine Lewis, James Menuge and Kim Phillips (Gloucester: Sutton, 1999).

4 Here, Margaret's status is important not only because it demonstrates her inherent nobility but because it highlights the different fates of noble women as opposed to slaves. In this case, however, there seems to be no other choice but wife or concubine. The possibility that she might refuse either proposition is never addressed.

5 The manuscript reads a fair "Margaret," this is a pun on her name since Marguerite means "pearl." This same pun is used in the legends of both Saint Pelagia and Saint Margaret Pelagia.

you will not consent to me, I shall have your body torn to pieces." Margaret replied, "My Lord Jesus Christ delivered himself to death for me, and therefore I do not dread to die for the love of Jesus Christ." Then the provost commanded that she be violently beaten until the blood ran off her as plentifully as a welling spring and then stretched out on the torture device known as the rack.[6] Those who were there wept and pleaded, "Margaret, truly we complain greatly to see you so piteously rent and torn apart. Alas, what beauty you have lost for your beliefs. Have pity on yourself so you may live." She said to them, "Oh you wicked counselors. Go away from me! This torment of the flesh is saving my soul!" Then she turned to the provost and said, "You shameless hound that cannot be satisfied. You may have power over my flesh, but God keeps my soul." The provost covered his face with his cloak so he would not see her blood shed in such great quantities.

After that, he had her locked in prison, but a marvelously bright light shone within. When she was in prison, she prayed to Our Lord to visibly show[7] her the one who so cruelly vexed her and fought against her. Suddenly a great dragon appeared before her. He attacked in order to devour her, but she made the sign of the cross and he vanished away. However, it is read elsewhere that he opened his mouth and swallowed her, but because she had made the sign of the cross the dragon suddenly burst and the virgin stepped out unscathed.[8]

The fiend came to her again, transformed into the figure of a man in order to deceive her. When she saw him she went to her knees in prayer, and when she rose, the fiend came to her, took her by the hand, and said, "Cease now, in regard to me, and satisfy yourself with what you have already done." Then she grabbed him by the hair, threw him to the ground, set her right foot upon his neck, and said, "Lie still under the foot of a woman, you enemy." She beat him until he cried out, "Ah blessed virgin Margaret, I am overcome. If a young man had beaten me I would not have given it a second thought. But I have been vanquished by a young, tender maid, and for that I am

6 The manuscript reads "Eculee," which is probably a colloquial term for the rack or perhaps a scribal error.

7 Here the scribe makes a point that Margaret wants something that she can see with her eyes as opposed to something that she "sees" with her heart as an extension of her faith. So God obliges her with the dragon.

8 Ryan's translation says this other version "is considered apocryphal and not to be taken seriously" (*The Golden Legend*, vol. 1, p. 369).

sorrowful because her father and mother have been my good friends." She restrained him so tightly and compelled him to tell her why he tempted Christian people so often. He answered that he harbored a deep hatred for them and all their virtues, and although he was often put back by them and despised by them, he pursued them with a continuous desire to deceive them. He envied the wealth of man because of the blessing he had lost and could not recover,[9] but he hoped to exclude them from it as well. Then he told her how Solomon had trapped a huge multitude of demons in a glass vessel.[10] But after his death, the demons sent firelight out of the vessel so men thought it contained great treasure and broke it open; the demons spilled out and filled the air. When he told her all of this, the virgin lifted her foot and said, "Flee, you wretched demon!" and he vanished. Her resolve was steadfast because he who overcomes the prince of evil may, without fail, easily defeat his minister.

The following day, the people gathered as she was presented before the judge. She refused to sacrifice to their gods, so they broiled her tender body with firebrands, and everyone marveled how such a tender maid could withstand so much torment. After that they bound her tightly and placed her in a vessel full of water in order to increase her pain by constantly changing the intensity of her torture. Suddenly the earth trembled, the air grew hideous, and the virgin emerged unharmed. Five thousand men were converted then and beheaded for the name of Jesus Christ. The provost feared that others would do the same, so he commanded hastily that the blessed virgin Margaret should be beheaded. She asked for time to pray for herself, her persecutors, and those who remembered her or asked devoutly

9 This is a reference to the account in the Old Testament Book of Isaiah of Lucifer's expulsion from heaven for his refusal to serve God. Isaiah 14: 11–14: "Thy pride is brought down to hell, thy carcass is fallen down: under thee shall the moth be strewed, and worms shall be thy covering. How art thou fallen from heaven, O Lucifer, who didst rise in the morning? How art thou fallen to earth, that didst wound the nations? And thou saidst in thy heart: I will ascend into heaven, I will exalt my throne above the stars of God, I will sit in the mountains of the covenant in the sides of the north. I will ascend above the height of the clouds, I will be like the most High."

10 In the apocryphal *Wisdom of Solomon*, Solomon entraps the demons in a bottle of brass. This may be a mistranslation or a scribal error. *The Testament of Solomon* in the Old Testament Apocrypha speaks of Solomon being given the authority, by God, to "confine all the demons both female and male." It is referred to as "an essay in popular demonology and magic" (*Apocryphal Old Testament*, ed. H. F. D. Sparks (Oxford: Clarendon Press, 1984), pp. 733, 738).

for her help. She devoutly prayed that any woman who asked for her help in childbirth would be delivered without peril to either the mother or child, and that both might be saved: the woman to life, the child to the kingdom of Christ.[11] As soon as she finished her prayer, a voice from heaven said that her prayers had been heard. She thanked Our Lord and said to her executioner, "Brother, take your sword and smite me." He struck off her head with one stroke, and so she received the crown of martyrdom. She suffered death the twelfth day of July. A holy man[12] spoke of Margaret in this manner: "The blessed Margaret was steadfast and stable in the love and fear of God, the worship of her religion; she was arrayed with compunction, and imbued with praiseworthy patience. Nothing contrary could be found in her; she was hateful to her father and friends but loved Our Lord Jesus Christ." Here ends the life of that blessed virgin Saint Margaret.

11 Margaret is asking to be the guardian of women in labor: to deliver both the woman and the child, either by saving the woman's life or by acting as the mediatrix between the child and God.

12 Jacobus never identifies this holy man, but Ryan suggests that it could be a reference to Ambrose's *On Virgins* (*The Golden Legend*, vol. 1, p. 368).

Saint Paula

This legend is extracted from Jerome's letter on the life of Saint Paula, in which he claims to have known her and witnessed all the miracles performed by her. All but a dozen or so words are from Jerome; it has been taken in "snippets," out of order, and is not nearly as long as Jerome's letter. According to Ryan, "Jacobus extracted paragraphs and snippets sufficient to establish Paula's sanctity by dwelling on the usual virtues – humility, charity, poverty, *contemptus mundi*, chastity. The 'snippets' are often taken out of context, which at times obscures the train of thought. Jerome's 'letter' is five or six times as long as Jacobus's chapter, and its rhetorical, eulogistic style is totally foreign to [Jacobus]."[1] The *Gilte Legende* scribe follows Jacobus's format and may never have seen Jerome's original.

Jerome wrote a series of letters discussing Saint Paula and her two daughters, Blesilla and Eustochium, both of whom were virgins. His letter on the death of Blesilla, to which he makes reference in the letter on Paula, is found in the *Patrologia Latina,* volume 22: 463, Epistles 38 and 39. Epistles 45 and 46 make reference to Paula and Eustochium (vol. 22: 480, 483); but the actual letter that Jacobus uses as his source is Epistle 108 (vol. 22: 878) addressed to her daughter Eustochium, virgin, and is titled "Epitaphium Paulae matris."

Paula's legend is one of contemplation, highlighted by her voluntary separation from her children and her severe lifestyle. She is the picture of marital obedience and motherly love until she forsakes her children to journey to the Holy Land. She dies peacefully, reciting passages from the Gospels that she has memorized and interpreted. Her spiritual understanding of the Scriptures is an example of the two different modes of learning – spiritual versus literal – that were developing in the early Christian period. Jerome's account of Paula's transformation and visions gives them credibility and sets her as an example of piety that was venerated throughout the Middle Ages.

1 William Granger Ryan, *The Golden Legend: Readings on the Saints* (Princeton: Princeton University Press, 1993) vol. 1, p. 121.

The Life of Saint Paula

Paula was a noble Roman lady, about whom Saint Jerome wrote the legend with these words:[2] "If all the members of my body turned into tongues so that they could speak with many voices, I could not say anything worthy of the virtues and holiness of the noble and worshipful Paula, who was noble of kin but much more noble by faith and by holiness, and at one time mighty in riches. But now she is more involved with the poverty of Jesus Christ. I witness in Jesus Christ and in his angels, and in the same angel who was companion and keeper of that marvelous woman, that I may not say anything sufficient about the grace of her, nor in the manner of her appraisers. But that which I have to say, I put forward as a witness of the least of her merits. And if the reader would know her virtues, she left everything to the poor. And just as among many stones the precious stone shines, and the brightness of the sun darkens and shadows the meager light of the stars, she so surmounted the virtues and the might of all by her humility. She was the least of all in order to be the greatest of all. For as much as she despised herself most, she was more enhanced by God. For in fleeing joy, she deserved joy, which follows virtue like a shadow and leaves him who covets it and sees him who despises it.

"This same woman had five children, including Blesilla,[3] upon the death of whom I comforted Paula in Rome; Pammachius, her heir and executor of her belongings, for whom we made a little book upon Paula's death;[4] Eustochium, who is now a precious jewel in the holy places in the church of virginity; and Rufina, who broke her mother's heart because she died without ripeness of age. After that, Paula would have stopped bearing children because she would no longer perform the office of marriage. But Paula obeyed the will of her

2 The rest of the legend is taken directly from Jacobus's adaptation of Jerome's letter and is therefore convoluted in places. I have tried to follow the text as closely as possible and still make it coherent.

3 I have used the forms of the children's names from Jerome's original text and Ryan's translation of the Latin instead of the Middle English forms in favor of consistency.

4 In Ryan, Pammachius is the husband of Paulina, and therefore Paula's son-in-law: "Paulina, who made Pammachius, her saintly and admirable husband, heir to all her property and projects, for whom I wrote a small book about her death" (*The Golden Legend*, vol. 1, p. 121). The Middle English scribe has listed Pammachius among Paula's children.

husband, who desired to have a male heir.[5] When her husband died, she wept so hard for him she nearly died from sorrow.

"She converted herself so much to the service of God that she desired to have the same death that he had. What more shall I say? She gave the great and noble houses and the great riches of before to the poor. She was so inflamed by the virtues of Paulinus, the bishop of Antioch, and of Epiphanius, who had come to Rome, that she decided to leave her own country. As I waited behind, her brother, her cousins, her friends, and, most of all, her own children followed her. But the sail was drawn up and the ship driven forth by the conduct of oars, and on the shore, little Toxocius[6] held up his hands, beseeching; and Rufina, who was about to be married, prayed for her mother to wait until after her wedding to leave and half died from weeping. But the whole time Paula held her eyes to heaven and toward Eustochium,[7] ignoring her children and putting her trust in God. She, unknowingly the servant of God, was tormented in her bowels,[8] as though men had drawn them out of her body. She fought with sorrow and suffered against the pains of her maternal nature. In that rejoicing, her courage coveted the love of her children as the greatest of its kind, yet she left them all for the love of God. She only comforted herself with Eustochium, who was her companion in her age. In the time that the ship sailed forth into the sea, all those who had been with her were beside the shore. She held her eyes to heaven and turned them from those whom she could not behold without sorrow and torment as she came to the Holy Land.

"The provost of Palestine knew well of her worthiness. Her people were sent before his men to array a great palace for her. But she chose a little cell and visited the holy places every day with such great study and so much fervor that if she had not been in such a hurry to go to the others, she would not have been drawn away from the first. When she kneeled before the cross, she worshiped in

5 This is a reference to her little son Toxocius, whom the scribe has not named. Ryan's text includes the child's name (*The Golden Legend*, vol. 1, p. 122).

6 The scribe has "the Thoroche," but again I follow Ryan's translation of "little Toxocius" for consistency.

7 The text reads "Fekonye," which is possibly a proper name, perhaps a form of "Eustoche," which is the name given by Jerome. I have followed Jerome.

8 The duties of wives and mothers are expounded in Saint Paul's epistle to the Colossians (Col. 3: 12–13): "Put ye on therefore, as the elect of God, holy and beloved, the bowels of mercy, benignity, humility, modesty, patience: Bearing with one another, and forgiving one another, if any have a complaint against another: even as the Lord hath forgiven you, so do you also."

beholding our Lord as though he hung upon it. When she entered into the sepulchre where he arose, she kissed the stone that the angel had taken away from the monument, she embraced the places where the holy body had lain, and she drew into her mouth the desired waters of belief that she coveted. All Jerusalem is witness to her weeping and the tears shed from her eyes, as is our Lord, himself, to whom she prayed.

"From there she went to Bethlehem and entered into the birthplace of our Savior and saw the holy place and swore, which I heard myself, that she saw with the eyes of her belief the child wrapped in swaddling clothes, weeping in the crib, and the kings worshiping our Lord, and the star shining upon the Virgin Mother, and the shepherds nourishing the beasts that came to see the Son of God who was made to die.[9]

"The beginning of John the Evangelist, which is: 'In the beginning was the word and the word was made flesh.'[10] She saw Herod in his anger slaying children,[11] Mary and Joseph fleeing into Egypt,[12] and Paula spoke in words mingled with tears, saying, 'God save the house of peace in Bethlehem in which the bread that descended from heaven was born. God save the entire plentiful country, about which plentitude David spoke in this manner: *Truly we shall enter within His tabernacles and worship the place where His feet stood.* And I, wretched sinner, am judged worthy to kiss the crib in which Our Lord cried very little and the pit in which the Virgin bore God. Here is my rest, here I shall dwell, I shall choose it as my Savior chose it before me.'

"She lived her life with such great humility that those who saw her and had seen her before in her great estate would not have believed that it was she, but that it was the lowest of her chambermaids

9 Matt. 2: 1–11 describes the Nativity, Massacre of the Innocents, Adoration of the Magi, and the Flight into Egypt.

10 The text reads: "In principo erat verbum et verbum caro factum est." The beginning of the Gospel of Saint John: "In the beginning was the Word, and the Word was with God, and the Word was God" (John 1: 1) This, however, appears to be an interpretation of that verse as opposed to a direct translation. Perhaps this is an indication of Paula's view on spiritual rather than literal belief, which Jerome discusses later in her legend. Ryan makes it clear in his translation of the Latin that Christ is identified as the Word (*The Golden Legend*, vol. 1, p. 122), whereas the Middle English obscures that identification, perhaps through a mistranslation of the original exemplar or a deliberate interpretation.

11 Matt. 2: 16.

12 Matt. 2: 13.

instead. When she was living in the fellowship of virgins, which she often did, she was the most humble of all in speech, dress, and actions. Since her husband was dead, she never ate with men and she never shared the company of men, unless they were holy and high as a bishop,[13] nor did she ever enter into a bath unless she was sick, nor have a soft bed, even if she had a grievous fever; instead, she lay on the hard ground with a blanket of haircloth, and that she considered her resting place. But her rest might be called her prayers that she performed night and day. She wept so much for her minor sins that men would have thought she was guilty of more grievous sins. As she was often taught by us to spare her eyes and keep them to the lesson of the Gospel, she said, 'The face should be troubled that I have so often painted with colors against the commandments of God. The body that had tended toward so many delights should be tormented, because weeping must recompense long laughing; and the soft, precious clothes of silk must be changed into the severity of haircloth. I, who would have pleased man and the world, desire now to please Jesus Christ. If I were to preach on the same chastity among so many virtues, it would be an outrage.'[14] When she was in Rome she was an example to all the ladies of the city because she behaved in such a way that she did not gain a reputation for evil words; there were none who dared blaspheme against her.

"I confess my error, that when she had abandoned herself too much to giving, I took her aside and related this saying of the apostle: 'It appertains you not to refresh others with your tribulation. But it must be an equality in time, so that it behooves to provide that thing that men would fain to do, they may not always do.'[15] I also said many other things to her, which she received with great shame and

13 Ryan says Paula did not dine with men *even* if they were bishops or holy men (*The Golden Legend*, vol. 1, p. 123). Perhaps the scribe noted the contradiction of Jerome's close association with Paula, or perhaps it was a mistranslation.

14 Paula's voice is striking here because, according to Jerome's account, she does not wish to be a hypocrite; she feels that she cannot preach about chastity because she was a married woman and did not remain a virgin. However, Ryan has this line, or a variation of it, spoken by Jerome: "If, among so many and such great virtues, I should wish to emphasize her chastity, such praise would seem superfluous" (*The Golden Legend*, vol. 1, p. 123). The Middle English scribe may have mixed up the speakers, believing the first person still referred to Paula.

15 2 Cor. 8: 13–14: "For I mean not that others should be eased, and you burthened, but by an equality. In this present time let your abundance supply their want, that their abundance also may supply your want, that there may be an equality." It is not a direct quotation, however.

few words. I call our Lord to witness that she did everything for Jesus Christ, and that she desired to die so poor that she would not leave one penny to her daughter; and for her own body at her last end she wished to be wrapped in a strong shroud. She said to me, when I asked her, 'I shall find men I know who will give me one. If a poor man has nothing from me that I may give, if he is dead, I will give him what I have received from others.'[16] She would not spend her money on stones that are transitory here on earth, but instead, those that are found above earth, of which, Saint John says in the Apocalypse, the city of the Great King is made.[17]

"She only took oil with her meat on the high feast days, and then just a little, so that one thing could be said about her; she abstained from wine, liquors, fish, milk, honey, and other things that were soft to taste, which some people think that in eating them, they are being abstemious. If they have filled their bellies, they think it a spiteful man who blames them. She was so devout that, because of the great burning of virtues within her, it seemed to some that she was half mad. When men said to her that the brain must be sustained and nourished, she answered, 'We have been made treasure, beholden to the world of angels and men, and so we are fools of Jesus Christ, and one of God's fools is wiser than many men.'[18] After our church, which she gave over to the governance of men,[19] she founded three churches and put within them three fellowships of virgins that she assembled from diverse provinces, and as many noble men and men of low birth.[20] They were separated during their work and their

16 This passage is slightly obscure. Ryan's translation reads: "But if one poor beggar should die because he does not receive from me what I can give him even if I have to use what belongs to someone else, who will be held accountable for his life?" (*The Golden Legend*, vol. 1, p. 124). The Middle English scribe has left off the end of the sentence.

17 Jerusalem as described by Saint John in Rev. 21, specifically Rev. 21: 19: "And the foundations of the wall of the city were adorned with all manner of precious stones. The first foundation was jasper; the second, sapphire; the third, a chalcedony; the fourth, an emerald."

18 1 Cor. 4: 9–10: "For I think that God hath set forth us apostles, the last, as it were men appointed to death: we are made a spectacle to the world, and to angels, and to men. We are fools for Christ's sake, but you are wise in Christ; we are weak, but you are strong; you are honorable, but we are without honor." 1 Cor. 1: 25: "For the foolishness of God is wiser than men; and the weakness of God is stronger than men."

19 According to Ryan, Paula founded the monasteries and gave them "over to be ruled by men" (*The Golden Legend*, vol. 1, p. 124).

20 This is a reference to the "double monastery" that Paula founded in Jerusalem

meals, but during psalms and Mass they were together. When they spoke together among themselves, Paula would reprimand them with soft words and break the flesh of the virgins doubly with fasting because she preferred that the stomach ache rather than the thoughts be dissolute, saying that the cleanliness of the body and clothing is filth to the soul, and the things that are nothing or trivial among men of the world are heavy and grievous among the religious. Although she gave all things of meat and flesh generously to the sick, she would take nothing for herself when she was sick, and in that she was not equal, for those things that she did for others out of pity, she turned to hardness for herself.

"I shall tell of my experiences. It happened in the strong, burning heat of July that she had a burning fever and men believed she would die, but she recovered by the mercy of God, so the physicians said she must drink small amounts of wine and not drink water, lest she develop dropsy.[21] I prayed to the blessed Bishop Epiphanius to bid her and enjoin her to drink wine because she had a wise and subtle mind. She felt it and smiled at him and the one who directed him to her. Whenever that blessed bishop came to her, exhorting her many times before he left her again, I asked her how she had done, and she answered, 'I have so much profited that with much pain I have steered this old man that I shall drink no wine.'[22]

"She was faithful to her husband and mild in weeping. She broke meekly with her sensuality, and against her children she was always in peril of death. When she made the sign of the cross on her forehead and on her breast, the impression of the cross protected her against motherly sorrow and assuaged it. She overcame the courage of the faithful mind; but the bowels of the mother were troubled, and so she was overcome by the frailty of the body.[23]

under the supervision of Jerome in AD 386 for both monks and nuns. Ryan describes them as three monasteries for three different groups of women from each social strata (*The Golden Legend*, vol. 1, p. 124); however the *Gilte Legende* scribe makes specific reference to men here.

21 This is the disease dropsy, or something similar, which involves serious fainting fits and may have been a mild form of epilepsy.

22 The Middle English scribe attributes this comment to Paula, whereas Ryan's translation reads: "I succeeded so well that she almost persuaded me, an old man, not to drink wine!" (*The Golden Legend*, vol. 1, p. 124).

23 The Middle English scribe has garbled the sense of Jacobus's version, perhaps because he had trouble with the Latin. Ryan's translation reads: "She bore grief patiently but was stricken by the deaths of those dear to her, particularly of her children; the loss of her spouse and her daughters brought her close to death. She made

"She held the Holy Scripture in great reverence, and though she loved the stories and said it was the foundation of truth, yet she followed more the spiritual understanding and she defended the edification of the soul.[24] She spoke another tongue that is not revealed to the envious. She learned Hebrew, which I learned in my youth with great pain and the hard sweat of pity, and always had to think about it so it would not leave me. Paula learned it in such a way that she sang all her psalms in Hebrew and sounded the words without any property of the Latin tongue, a trait that we also see to this day in Eustochium, her daughter. We have up to this time driven our ship by good winds, and our ship has traversed the passing waters of the sea in running, and now our story runs into the rocks and shoals that are little ships. What is he who could tell of Paula's death without weeping? She became very feeble and desired to leave us in order to be more plainly with our Lord. Why do I abide so long and draw out my sorrow in abiding in other things? It is this way among women; she felt her death, and a part of her body and her limbs became cold, and she only felt her breath moving at her holy breast to pass forth a little.

"Then she softly said this verse: 'Lord I have loved the beauty of your house and the habitation of your glory.'[25] And then she said, 'Lord of virtues, how much I have coveted your beloved tabernacles. My soul fails in the being of my Lord. I have chosen to be despised in the house of my God rather than dwell in the tabernacles of sinners.'[26] And when I asked her why she held herself still and why she didn't answer my crying and sorrowing, she answered me in

the sign of the cross on her lips and her breast, hoping by that sign to ease the sorrow she felt as a wife and mother, but she was overcome by her emotion, and the mother's inner pain disturbed her believing soul. Conquering by strength of spirit, she was conquered by the fragility of the body" (*The Golden Legend*, vol. 1, p. 125).

24 Jerome differentiates between the spiritual understanding of the Scriptures, which depends more on the emotional interpretation of religious texts, and the literal understanding, which views the Scriptures as the Word of God to be followed in every detail, closely and literally. Paula follows the spiritual interpretation, which may explain why her biblical quotations are not verbatim. This idea of spiritual understanding is similar to that of the Gnostics, who had a more emotional "knowledge" of God. We will see this idea of gnosis again in the text of Mary Magdalene.

25 Ps. 25: 8: David's prayer to God in his distress: "I have loved, O Lord, the beauty of thy house and the place where thy glory dwelleth."

26 Ps. 83: 2, 11: "How lovely are thy tabernacles . . . I have chosen to be an abject in the house of my God, rather than to dwell in the tabernacles of sinners."

Greek that she had no sorrow because she felt that all things were transitory. Then she repeated this verse with her eyes closed until she yielded up her soul with such a quiet voice that I could hardly understand her.

"There was not a monk hidden in his desert cell nor any virgin who faithfully kept the secret places of her chamber who did not know that it would be a sacrilege not to attend the Mass when Paula was worshipfully laid in the grave beside the church. And Eustochium, her worshipful virgin daughter, could not be drawn from her mother, kissing her and always keeping her eyes to Paula's face, embracing her body, and she would have been buried with her mother. God is witness that she never left a penny to her daughter but left many to strangers, and it is more wondrous that she left money to a great multitude of brothers and sisters who were hard to sustain and it would have been wicked to turn away. Our Lord save you, Paula; help, I pray you, the old age of him, your worshiper." Here ends the life of Saint Paula.

Saint Elizabeth of Hungary

As one of the latest additions to the *Legenda Aurea*, the life of Saint Elizabeth (1207–31) is a striking picture of how the idea of sanctity shifted from the vocal virgin saints of the early Christian period to the pious ideal of the Middle Ages. Elizabeth is a historical figure, the daughter of the king of Hungary and wife of the son of Hermann, landgrave[1] of Thuringia; however, Jacobus does not give any clues to the identity of his source, though it was most likely a monk or priest in a house dedicated to Elizabeth, perhaps even in Mainz where a great number of her miracles took place. The version in the *Gilte Legende* is much shorter than that of the *Legenda Aurea*. Several of the miracles performed by Elizabeth have been omitted, as well as a number of her speeches and dialogues. The scribe of British Library MS Harley 630, perhaps in the interests of space or the desire to leave his own mark on the text, reordered a great deal of the legend, so at times it does not follow in chronological sequence. However, the basic facts of her life remain the same: she was married at fourteen, after being betrothed from the age of four, widowed at twenty, and lived an austere life until her death at the age of twenty-four in 1231.[2]

Elizabeth was noted for her acts of generosity and her conversion to saintly ideals early in life, and she was especially venerated by the Franciscans, in whose order she was a tertiary. Her story is one of obedience and meek compliance; her life is ruled by the men in it, particularly her confessor Conrad, who controls not only her actions but also the manifestation of her faith. She relinquishes all control over herself and her faith to a man described as a "lowly beggar" who resorts to beating her when she doesn't comply with his wishes or pay him enough reverence. Elizabeth is an example of how, in the Middle Ages, the idea of women's sanctity was often controlled by their male counterparts; their voices were filtered through the pens of male scribes who had their own agenda in creating an exemplar for

1 A minor land-owning noble.

2 Gaston Duchet-Suchaux and Michel Pastoureau, *The Bible and the Saints* (New York: Flammarion, 1994) p. 136.

women, religious and secular.[3] Conrad's dominance over Elizabeth, his influence on her lifestyle, and the severity with which she follows his lead illustrate an idea of how good women were meant to behave, forsaking the trappings of worldly eminence for the promise of heavenly glory. While the scribe omits a number of her greater miracles, he does not leave out the criticism leveled at Elizabeth for being a "waster of goods" when she doles out the resources of her husband's kingdom to the poor. Nor does he omit certain comments about Conrad that could be seen as less than complimentary, especially when he punishes Elizabeth for certain transgressions. Conrad wields his power like a secular tyrant, power that Elizabeth adopts herself in dealing with those she would convert, even against their will – as in the case of Radegund. So while Elizabeth is the picture of abject humility, she is given a forceful voice in bending others to Christian poverty and a certain power in determining the course of her own life.

Elizabeth stands as an example of holy motherhood precisely because her children do not play any role in her life, according to her biographer, and their absence is more resounding than their presence. They are mentioned only to illustrate that she has made a choice: to sacrifice her children for the love of God and holy poverty. Unlike Paula, she does not leave her children; she sends them away. Also unlike Paula, there is no mention of her experiencing pain at the separation until later when it serves to heighten her sanctity. Her children exist in negative; they are an impediment to her chosen path in life and subsequently are put away. In her compassion for strangers, Elizabeth becomes cold toward those close to her; she convinces her husband to leave on a crusade, sends her children away, and allows Conrad to separate her from her childhood companions so that all her attention is turned to God. She is most venerated for her charitable works, but these do not figure as prominently in her legend as her decision to sacrifice her secular life for her religious one. She is commended for making that choice and rejecting her societal role in favor of the ascetic life. This is how she lives and dies, but unlike her earlier, virgin successors, Elizabeth dies peacefully in her sleep without the crown of martyrdom. She is still received as a bride of Christ because she tortured herself through her

3 For more on how Elizabeth's legend highlights the tensions between religious and secular values see Dyan Elliott, "Dress as Mediator between Inner and Outer Self: the Pious Matron of the High and Later Middle Ages," *Mediaeval Studies* 53 (1991) pp. 279–308.

austerity and denial of earthly comforts, starving herself, exhausting herself, exposing herself to contagious disease, and subsisting in physical filth but spiritual purity.

The Life of Saint Elizabeth of Hungary

Saint Elizabeth was the daughter of the noble king of Hungary, and if she was noble by kindred, she was much nobler by faith and religion. She embellished her noble kindred by example and cleaned it by miracles; she enhanced it by the grace of holiness because the author of nature lifted her up in a manner above nature.

When this maid, nourished in real delights, renounced all childishness and put herself fully in the service of God, it appeared clearly how her tender childhood was enforced with simplicity and how she began her sweet devotion. From then on she began to costume herself in good manners and despise the plays of vanity, flee the prosperity of the world, and profit in all ways in the worship of God. When she was only five years old, she would attentively abide in the church in order to pray until her companions and servants took her away. When she met with any of her playmates, she would lead them as though it were a game toward the chapel, so that she would have reason to enter the church. When she entered, she would kneel down and lie flat on the pavement, and even though at that time she had no knowledge of letters, she would often open the Psalter before her and pretend to read and act as though no one should disturb her because she was occupied.

When she was playing with the other maidens of her estate, she would consider the manner in which they played so that she could always worship God on that occasion. When they played the rings and other games, she always set her sovereign trust and hope in God, and of all that she won or had in any other manner, she being a young maid, she gave the tenth part to poor maidens and often led them in saying the *Pater Noster*, and she often led them into the church to greet Our Lady. As she increased in age over time, she increased in devotion because she chose the Virgin Mary, mother of God, as her sovereign lady and advocate, and she chose Saint John the Evangelist as the keeper of her virginity.

On one occasion, there were scrolls laid upon the altar, and on each was written the name of an apostle. Each maiden chose one randomly, but Elizabeth prayed and three times she chose the scroll she desired, on which was written the name of Saint Peter, to whom she had such great devotion that she denied nothing to any creature who asked for something in his name. So that the good fortune of the world should not deceive her, she gave away some of her possessions every day. As soon as she took pleasure in any game, she would leave the remnant, saying that she did not lust for play any longer. But she would say to her fellowship, "I leave the remnant for God." She never went to festivals gladly but withdrew as much as she could. She always dreaded to wear fresh clothes and loved to go honestly. She made herself say a certain number of prayers, and if she was so occupied that she could not say them, or if she was constrained by her women to go to bed, she would wake and say them to God in her bed. This holy maid worshiped all the solemn days so greatly that she would not allow anyone to lace her sleeves for any occasion until the solemnity of the Mass was done and fulfilled. She heard the office of the church with such great reverence that when the Gospel was read, or when the host was lifted up, she would take off her gold brooches and the circlet from her head and lay them on the ground.

In the meantime, as she kept her virginity with great holiness, she was forced into marriage by her father, who greatly desired to reap the fruit of her youth, notwithstanding that it was completely against her will. But she did not dare refute the commandment of her father. Then she vowed to God and told this truth to Conrad, a holy man who was her confessor, that if she outlived her husband she would keep perpetual constancy. She was wedded to the landgrave of Thuringia as the royal might would have it. Divine law ordained that she should bring many of her people to the love of God. She was so fervent in prayer that she would go privately to the church before any of her men so that she might, by her secret prayers, achieve the grace of God. She would often rise at night to pray when her husband heartily prayed her to lie still. She arranged to have a lady who was more familiar with her than anyone else take her by the foot and softly wake her if she were overtaken by sleep and missed her hour. So one time, by chance, this lady meant to take her by the foot but took her husband by the foot instead. He awoke suddenly, considered this for what it was, and wisely let it pass.

Because she offered good sacrifice to God with her prayers, she often wet her body with an abundance of tears, and she shed them joyously, and often without changing any semblance of her expression she wept with sorrow. She was of such great humility that, for the love of God, she laid a sick man with a horrible face and stinking head into her lap. She washed his face and cleaned all the filth from his head, whereupon her women laughed at her in scorn. During the Rogation Days, she always followed the procession barefoot, clad in wool, and during the preaching she would sit with poor people. She would not adorn herself with precious stones, as others did, on the day of purification,[4] nor clothe herself with cloth of gold. But following the example of the Virgin Mary, with her son in her arms she offered a lamb and a candle meekly, thereby showing that the baubles and japes of the world were to be put away. When she went home, she gave the clothes she had worn that day to a poor woman. She was of such great humility that, with the consent of her husband, she put herself under the dominion of Master Conrad,[5] a poor man of little degree. But he was of noble substance in the perfect religion, so that she did whatever he commanded with joy and reverence, and in order to achieve the merits of obedience and of God, she was obedient until her death.

One time, it happened that Conrad called her to hear his preaching at the same time as the marquis of Losenge[6] came to visit, so she could not go to Mass. Her confessor felt that he was not well served because she did not release herself from her previous obligation, so she was stripped down to her smock, along with some of her women who were guilty with her, and he had them all beaten.

She was so abstinent that when she sat with her husband at meals, royally served with many dishes, the simple bread was sufficient for her. She was so rigorous that she lay pale and lean, but Master Conrad defended her for not touching any of her husband's meat against her conscience. Elizabeth kept his commandment with such great diligence that when others abounded in delicacies, she ate the common boiled meat with her chambermaids.

4 Ryan translates this as "churching," when a woman goes to church after childbirth to offer thanksgiving and receive a special blessing purifying her after the birth. William Granger Ryan, *The Golden Legend: Readings on the Saints* (Princeton: Princeton University Press, 1993) vol. 2, p. 305. This is the first reference to Elizabeth's children, and the scribe does not go into any detail about them. This episode is highlighted only because of her humility during the ceremony, not because of her role as a mother.

5 This version does not, as in Ryan, specify that Elizabeth gives herself to Conrad "with the marital right safeguarded" (*The Golden Legend*, vol. 2, p. 305). It may be an omission due to mistranslation from the Latin, or the scribe may have left it out to show how deeply Elizabeth was under Conrad's control.

6 Ryan mentions a "marchioness of Meissen," not a "marquis of Losenge" (*The Golden Legend*, vol. 2, p. 305).

One time, when she was traveling and was worn out from the journey, they brought her husband diverse meats that were won in true conquest,[7] but she refused them and took her refection of hard bread tempered with water. Because of this, her husband opposed her, so she lived with her chambermaids who consented to her purpose. Her husband suffered everything in patience and said that he would gladly live in the same manner if he were not afraid of the complaints of his people. She who was in the state of sovereign worship and glory coveted the state of sovereign poverty so that the world would have no part in her life and she would be very poor like Our Lord Jesus Christ. When she was alone with her chambermaids, she would clothe herself in vile clothing, set an old, poor veil on her head, and say, "Lo, this is how I will dress when I am a widow."[8] And though she was abstemious and strict with herself, she was free and generous to the poor, so much so that she would not suffer anyone living around her to be in need but gave generously to them all because she intended to perform all the seven works of mercy.

Once, Elizabeth gave a poor woman a beautiful piece of clothing, and when this poor woman saw that she had received such a noble gift, she delighted in it so much that she fell down to the earth as though she were dead. When the blessed Elizabeth saw this, she sorrowed greatly that she had given her such a noble gift, dreading that she had caused this woman's death. Then Elizabeth prayed for her and she arose perfectly well. Many times Elizabeth would spin wool[9] with her chambermaids, and she would make cloth so that, by

7 Ryan has "might not have been honestly acquired" (*The Golden Legend*, vol. 2, p. 305). The scribe's implication is that the meat was honestly won but that Elizabeth would still not touch it.

8 Ryan says "when I have attained the state of poverty," which highlights the financial status versus the marital status (*The Golden Legend*, vol. 2, p. 306).

9 Spinning wool is a symbol of Elizabeth's humility; embroidering with silk was the usual occupation of the aristocracy, while spinning wool, since it was a necessity, was the occupation of serving women and peasants. Cf. *Piers Plowman*: "And ye lovely ladies with youre longe fyngres,/ That ye have silk and sandel to sowe whan tyme is/ Chesibles for chapeleyns chirches to honoure./ Wyves and widewes, wolle and flex spynneth:/ Maketh cloth, I counseille yow, and kenneth so youre doughtres./ The nedy and the naked, nymeth hede how thei liggeth,/ And casteth hem clothes, for so comaundeth Truthe./ For I shal lenen hem liflode, but if the lond faille,/ As longe as I lyve, for the Lordes love of hevene./ And alle manere of men that through mete and drynke libbeth,/ Helpeth hym to werche wightliche that

her own labor that she gave to the churches, she might receive glorious fruits and set a good example to others.

During a time when her husband, the landgrave, was away at the court of the Emperor Frederick of Cremona, she assembled all the wheat of the year in a garner and ministered to everyone who arrived from all parts of the kingdom, for there was a great shortage throughout the entire country. Many times when silver money failed her, she would sell all her jewels and clothes to give to the poor, but no matter what she gave, the grain stores were never depleted of the corn that was in them. She built a great house at the base of the castle where she could receive and nourish a great multitude of poor people. Every day she visited them, sparing nothing and braving the corruption of evil air and foul sickness, washing them and wiping them with her own hands and her own kerchief when she had nothing else. She also nourished the children of poor women in that house so benignly that they all called her mother. She made the sepulchres for the poor people when they died, went devoutly to their deathbed, and helped bury them with her own hands in cloth that she had made, and many times she would bring her own sheets to bury the dead bodies in.

Among all these things, her husband's devotion should be highly praised, for even though he was always occupied, he was always devout in the service of God. For as much as he could not personally attend to spiritual things, he gave his wife power to do all that she could in the worship of God and for the health of souls. The blessed Elizabeth greatly desired that her husband should leave all worldly occupations and with all his power and might go and defend the faith of God. She entreated him with meek and devout prayers to go visit the holy land, and he virtuously applied himself to goodness and went there. When he was there, that noble, true, and devout prince, full of faith and devotion, yielded up his spirit to Our Lord God and received the glorious fruit of his works. Then she, with great devotion, received the state of widowhood. When the death of her husband was published throughout Frisia,[10] some of her husband's retainers felt that she was nothing more than a fool and a waster of goods, so they cruelly disinherited her.

wynneth youre foode." William Langland, *The Vision of Piers Plowman*, ed. A. V. C. Schmidt. (London: Everyman, 1998) the B text, passus 6, ll.10–20, pp. 95–6.

10 It is Ryan who names the country as Thuringia. I have left the name as it appears in the manuscript.

Because of that, her wisdom was clearer and she could be certain of the poverty she long desired, so she went by night to a poor man's house and lay among the hogs. She gave thanks to God with all her heart and at matins she went to a monastery of the Friars Minor[11] and asked them to thank God for her tribulation. The following day, she came to the place and house of her enemy with her little children, and he delivered her to a severe place to live in. And when she saw how much her host and hostess were against her, she greeted and kissed the walls saying, "I would fain take my leave of men, but I find none."[12] So, constrained by necessity, she sent her young children here and there to be cared for in diverse places[13] and then returned to the poor man's house where she had first slept. On her way there, she had to use a narrow path that could only be passed on stepping-stones, and the mire all around and under them was foul and deep. As she passed, she met an old woman for whom she had done many good things, but the woman would not let her pass and instead, shoved her into the mire, and she fell down into the deepest part of the muck. But as was her nature, she got up, wiped her clothes, and laughed. One time she was persistently asked by a group of religious[14] to visit their cloister, and she went without the permission of her confessor. When she came home again, he had her beaten so cruelly that even after three weeks the traces were still there.

She was of such great humility that she would not allow her chambermaids to address her as "lady" but insisted that they address her as the least and lowest person in her household. Sometimes she would wash the dishes and the vessels of the kitchen and hide them so her chambermaids would not find them before she could do it saying, "If I could have found a more despicable life, I would have chosen it." She chose the better part, as Mary did; she believed in spiritual grace through shedding tears, seeing heavenly visions, and enflaming others with the love of God.[15] During Lent, when she was in the

11 Franciscans.

12 Elizabeth desires to live a solitary life, possibly as a tertiary, but has been more or less imprisoned and kept from her desires.

13 So, like Paula, Elizabeth abandons her children in favor of spiritual love and devotion, but, unlike Paula, her children are anonymous, further diminishing their importance to their mother.

14 Ryan translates this as "nuns," but the *Gilte Legende* does not make specific reference to gender.

15 This is a reference to the life of Mary Magdalene, but parallels can also be drawn with the life of Saint Mary of Egypt, who was visited by heavenly visions, lifted

church, she gazed intensely at the altar as though her mind had been ravished. At this time, she was comforted and replenished by divine revelation. She then returned to her house and prophesied that she would see Jesus Christ in heaven, and anon she lay down in her woman's lap out of feebleness and began to look up toward heaven; she felt such great joy that she began to laugh heartily. When she had endured this gladness a great while, she suddenly started weeping; then she looked up to heaven again and was restored to her earlier joy. When she closed her eyes she began to weep, and she carried on like this until compline, abiding in divine visions, and then she held her peace awhile. Afterward she said, "Ah Lord, will you be with me and I with you, Lord; I will never part from you." Then after that, her chambermaids asked her why she had laughed and then wept like that. She replied, "I saw the heavens open and my Lord Jesus Christ inclined toward me. I was glad of that vision and wept when we parted. And he said to me, 'If you will be with me, I shall be with you.' And I answered as you heard."

Her prayers were so virtuous that she drew others to God, as it appears, because of a young man whom she called to her and said, "You live a desolate life. Would you like me to pray to God for you?" And he replied, "I would, gladly, and I require it." And then she began to pray with the young man. After a while the young man began to cry out, "Cease, good lady, cease!" But she continued to pray more fervently, and he began to cry, "Cease lady for I fail so much I burn." He was seized with such an intense heat that he was sweating and smoking. He cast his clothes from himself like a mad man, throwing his arms out as though he were out of his mind. Men ran to him and helped him undress. The heat that emanated from him was so intense that they could not endure to touch him; then it subsided and he came to his senses. After this he entered into the Order of the Friars Minor.

An abbess who was Elizabeth's kin had great compassion for her poverty and took her to her uncle, a bishop, who received her with great joy, fully intending to marry her off again. When a gentlewoman who had vowed chastity with her heard his purpose, she told it with great weeping and sorrow to her lady Elizabeth, who comforted her and said, "Trust in Our Lord, for the love of whom I have avowed perpetual chastity. He will keep my counsel and though

into the air by angels, and fed with manna. Elizabeth covets their experiences and has visions of her own.

my uncle would offer me in marriage, I shall dissent with my soul and speak against him with my words. And if I see no other remedy, I shall cut off my own nose and make myself so deformed that every man will be disgusted by me."[16] As she was sent against her will to the bishop's castle to wait until he had arranged a marriage for her, she recommended her chastity to God with weeping and tears.

In the meantime, by the ordinance of God, the bones of her husband were brought from beyond the sea, and the bishop sent for her immediately so she could devoutly meet them. Then she and the bishop received these bones in a solemn procession with great devotion and shedding of tears. Then she turned to her God and said, "I give you thanks, my Lord God, that you will vouchsafe in order to comfort me, your wretched creature, with the bones of my dear husband. You know, Lord, that I loved you, and for your love I forsook his presence gladly and stirred him to go to the Holy Land. And though it would have been delightful for me to have lived with him and gone begging in the poorest way throughout the world, I bear witness to you that I would not be with him again against your will for the least of the hairs on my head, nor would I call for him to be a mortal man again. Therefore, Lord, I commend both him and me fully to your grace." Then, so she would not lose the hundredfold fruit given to those who keep the perfection of the Gospel, she took the clothing of religion which she chose to be rude, foul, and abject, keeping perpetual chastity after the death of her husband, embracing perfect obedience and willful poverty. Her habit was despicable, her mantle of the foulest russet, her gown another vile color, her sleeves torn and clotted with old cloth. Her father, the king of Hungary, saw how his daughter had fallen into such mischief and need, so he sent an earl to bring her home to her native country. When the earl arrived, he found her sitting meekly in the simplest attire, spinning. For shame, confusion, and great wonder, he cried out, "Alas, who ever saw a king's daughter sit in such a vile habit and perform such a foul occupation as spinning wool." As he labored with all his power to bring her home to her father, she would not consent, saying that she would rather live in abject poverty than abound in all the riches of the world so that her soul could pass to God with no impediments to

16 Saint Paula threatens to cut off her nose to spite her face, like the Anglo-Saxon Saint Frideswithe. See Jane Tibbetts Schulenberg, "The Heroics of Virginity: Brides of Christ and Sacrificial Mutilation" in *Women in the Middle Ages and Renaissance*, ed. Mary Beth Rose (Syracuse, N.Y.: Syracuse University Press, 1986).

her devotion. She prayed to God that he would put disdain in her heart toward all temporal things and withdraw the love of her children from her heart so that she could, with a sad and stable heart, be content with all tribulation and affliction. When she finished her prayers, she said to her servants, "Our Lord has heard my prayer because I account all temporal things as nothing more than filth and mire, and I love my children no more than the children of other men, and I fear no pain nor reprieve nor despite, and now I feel that I do not desire nor love anything but God."[17]

Her confessor, Master Conrad, often put heavy and contrary burdens upon her, and whatever it seemed that she loved most she would eliminate from her fellowship, including two young men, good and true, who had been nourished with her since childhood, and there were many tears shed on both sides. But Conrad did this to break her will so that she would address all her affection to God and so that none of her servants would bring her mind back to her former worldly glory. In all these things she was gladly obedient and steadfastly patient so that she could possess her own soul by patience and be beautified by the victory of obedience. She would often say, "If I dread mortal man as much as the love of God, I am much more bound to fear God, the heavenly judge, and therefore I have chosen to be obedient to a poor beggar, my Master Conrad, instead of rich bishops so that I may utterly cut from me all the comforts of temporal things."

She was continuously occupied with works of mercy. Five hundred marks were delivered to her as her dower, and she gave half to the poor, and with the other half she built a hospital; because of that she was called a waster of goods, and they all called her a lewd fool, but she humbly and gladly suffered all these injuries and tribulations. When the hospital was built, she ordained herself as the servant of all the poor people in the hospital, and she bore herself so humbly and so meekly in this service that by night she would bear the sick people to the privy to ease them and then bear them to their beds again. She washed their clothes and cleansed all the filth and vermin from them; she looked after lepers, washed them and wiped their wounds, and did everything herself that belonged to hospitality. And when she had no poor people to minister to, she would

17 In this speech, Elizabeth mentally abandons the children that she had already physically abandoned. This is the last of three references to her children in the entire legend, which underscores her devotion to God and the sacrifice of her maternal nature.

spin wool that was sent by her to a nearby abbey and gave the price of it to the poor.

When she had abided a long time in great poverty, she received another five hundred marks from her dower, which she properly distributed to the poor. She made an ordinance that whoever left their place in line at the expense of another while she was giving out her alms would have their hair cut off. By chance, a maid named Radegund, who had wondrously beautiful hair, walked by. She passed there, not to receive alms, but to visit her sister who was sick. But she was brought to Saint Elizabeth as a violator of the ordinance, and Elizabeth commanded that she should cut off her hair, and the maid wept and protested as much as she could. When a man there said she was innocent, Saint Elizabeth said, "She will not go to harvest festivals or carols to show off her hair."[18] Then Saint Elizabeth asked her if she had ever thought of living a life of healing, and she answered that if she didn't love her hair so much she would have taken the habit of religion a long time before. Saint Elizabeth said, "I would rather you lost your hair than have my own son made emperor." Immediately the maid took the habit of religion.

When the time that God had ordained neared for her who despised the mortal kingdom for that of angels, she laid down in her bed, turned toward the wall, and those who were there beheld her and heard a sweet melody coming from her. One of her chambermaids asked her what it was; she answered and said, "A bird has come between me and the wall, and he sings so sweetly that he moves me to sing as well." In that sickness, she was always happy and in prayer. The last day of her passing, she asked her women, "What will you do?" The devil appeared, and she began to cry three times, "Flee! Flee!" as she chased the fiend away. Then she said, "Midnight nears, at which time my Lord Jesus Christ was born. It is the time that my Lord God calls his friends to his wedding." Then our Lord Jesus Christ appeared to her saying, "Come, my beloved and enter into the tabernacle of your Lord God." In this manner she slept in our Lord, the year of our Lord 1227.[19] At that time, the greatest multitude of birds that had ever been seen landed upon the church. They began to sweetly sing a melody that was so great no heart could imagine what

18 This is a reference to the seasonal festivals and ring dances that were often held at harvest time or at the beginning of summer.

19 Ryan has 1231. Either the scribe miscopied the date from his exemplar or the date was mixed up through multiple redactions (*The Golden Legend*, vol. 2, p. 313).

it might be, and it seemed as though they came to sing a mass for her. Though her body lay four days on the earth before she was buried, she was always full of sweetness and untouched by decay. Then her body was laid in a monument that afterwards welled oil, and many fair miracles were performed at her tomb after her death.

In the region of the diocese of Saxony, there was a monk called Homer,[20] who became so sick that he cried out and would not allow anyone near him to sleep. One night a worshipful lady clothed in white appeared to him and bade him to vow himself to Saint Elizabeth in order to be healed. The following night she appeared again, and by the counsel of his abbot he made his vow. The third night she appeared to him and made the sign of the cross on his shoulder, and he was restored to perfect health. When the abbot and the prior came to him, they marveled greatly and dreaded the fulfillment of this vow because the prior said that often, under the guise of good, illusions of the enemy come. So they counseled him to confess his vow and retract it. The following night, the same person appeared to him and said, "You shall always be sick until you have performed your vow." Instantly his sickness overtook him again, but by the license of his abbot he fulfilled the vow and was made perfectly whole.

A maiden asked her servant for a drink, and the servant took her the drink and said, "The devil must you drink." As she drank it felt as though a burning fire entered into her body, and she swelled up as great as a barrel so that everyone could see that she was possessed by a demon. She was in this state for two years, but then she was led to the tomb of Saint Elizabeth and was cured.

Herman, a man from the diocese of Tholose, was being held in prison, and with great devotion he called on Saint Elizabeth to help him. The following night she appeared to him and comforted him greatly. The next day, sentence was given against him and he was hanged. The judge gave his kindred leave to take him down; then they carried his body and prayed to Saint Elizabeth, and he was resurrected before them all.

A child fell into a well and drowned. Someone came to draw water from the well, found him dead, and drew him out. Then he vowed the child to Saint Elizabeth, and he was restored to life. Another maid

20 At a monastery in the diocese of Hildersheim, Saxony, there was a Cistercian monk named Henry (Ryan, *The Golden Legend*, vol. 2, p. 313).

also drowned, and she was brought back to life again by Elizabeth's merits.

Frederick, who was cunning in the craft of swimming, was bathing in water and scorned a poor man to whom Elizabeth had given sight. Then the poor man said, "That holy lady who has done me grace will avenge me so that you will never come out of the water alive." And immediately the swimmer lost his strength and could not help himself, so he sank down to the bottom like a stone, and was drowned and pulled out dead. Then some of his neighbors pledged him to Saint Elizabeth, and carried him on a seven-day journey in her direction, and she gave him life again.

Theodrik was grievously sick in his knees and thighs so he could not walk. He vowed that he would seek the tomb of Saint Elizabeth. He was there a month, found no remedy, and went back to his house. One night in his sleep he thought that a man sprayed water on him. He woke angry and said, "Why have you thrown water on me?" The man said, "I have wet you. Believe that this wetting shall be helpful to you." Then instantly Theodrik rose completely healed and gave thanks to God and Saint Elizabeth. Here ends the life of Saint Elizabeth, the daughter of the king of Hungary.

Mary Magdalene

The legend of Mary Magdalene has its roots in the Bible and is a compilation of a number of segments of the Gospels, including: Mary Magdalene as the witness to Christ's Resurrection; the sinful woman who repents and washes Christ's feet with her hair; and the sinful woman from whom Christ drives the seven devils. Jacobus's version also incorporates many aspects of the legend of Mary of Egypt, including her thirty-year sojourn into the desert.

In AD 591 Gregory the Great combined the three Marys of the Gospel into one saint, a composite saint who is identified by all of those traits and stands out as a shining example of the power of salvation.[1] This is how she was viewed throughout the Middle Ages, when she was venerated second only to the Virgin Mary as an intercessor for men and a key to redemption for women who were tainted by the sin of Eve. Her role as a preacher in this text is so important because she has her own voice and her own authority. Mary Magdalene is also the prime figure in the Gnostic text *The Gospel According to Mary*, which highlights her role in disseminating the word of God and the news of the Resurrection. Her position as a preacher is challenged by Peter, just as the Gnostic view of Christianity, one that focuses on the *knowledge* of God, was challenged by the Catholic Church.[2] She becomes the *apostolorum apostola*, apostle of the apostles; a role she exemplifies in the version of her life found in the *Legenda Aurea* and the *Gilte Legende*. Jacobus mentions other sources for his rendition, such as the treatises of Hegesippus (or Josephus) and a Gospel of John by a Brother Albert, who may have been Saint Albert the Great (OP), an older contemporary of Jacobus.

Most of the material in the legend of Mary Magdalene is apocryphal and appears in various forms throughout the Middle Ages, most notably, however, in the Digby Play of Mary Magdalene, of which the *Gilte Legende* may have been a source. This version of *Mary*

1 Katherine Ludwig Jansen, *The Making of the Magdalen: Preaching and Popular Devotion in the Later Middle Ages* (Princeton: Princeton University Press, 2000) p. 33.

2 Jansen, *The Making of the Magdalen*, p. 24.

Magdalene is in Trinity College, Dublin Library MS 319, though it belongs to the fragment containing part of the *Gilte Legende* and is distinct from the *Dorothy/Catherine* fragment that is bound with it.

The Life of Mary Magdalene

Mary Magdalene's surname was taken from Magdala Castle, and she was born of the kindred descended from royal kings. Her father was called Syrus, and her mother Eucharia. Mary and Lazarus, her brother, and Martha, her sister, owned the castle two miles from Nazareth and Bethany, near Jerusalem, and they owned a great part of Jerusalem. They divided these holdings between them in such a way that Mary had Magdala, for which she was named; Lazarus had the part of Jerusalem; and Martha had Bethany.

While Mary Magdalene was enjoying all the delights of the body, their brother Lazarus inclined most toward knighthood, and Martha, who was wise, governed the holdings of her brother and sister and ministered to the needs of two knights, two servants, and two poor men. They sold all their holdings after the ascension of our Lord and brought the proceeds from the sale to the apostles' feet. Mary Magdalene abounded greatly in riches and wealth, and the delight that is fellow to an abundance of possessions. Inasmuch as she shone with beauty and riches, so much more had she subjected her body to delights; therefore she lost her proper name and was customarily called a sinful woman.

When our Lord preached here on earth, she was inspired by grace and went to the house of Simon the Leper when our Lord dined there. She did not dare to appear among the righteous men, for she was sinful, but she came to the feet of our Lord and there she washed them with her tears, wiped them with her hair, and anointed them with precious ointments,[3] for the dwellers of that land used baths and ointments because of the heat of their homeland. Because of this, Simon thought to himself that if our Lord were a true prophet, he would not suffer to let a sinful woman touch him. Therefore our Lord, with true pride, forgave the woman all her sins.[4] This is Mary

3 Luke 7: 36–50.

4 It is unusual that "true pride" is used in reference to Mary's forgiveness; it may be a mistranslation made by the Middle English scribe. In Ryan, Simon is the one referred to as being proud. William Granger Ryan, *The Golden Legend: Readings on the Saints* (Princeton: Princeton University Press, 1993) vol. 1, p. 376.

Magdalene, to whom our Lord gave so many great gifts and showed so many great tokens of love that he drove demons out of her[5] and set her afire with his love and made her truly familiar with him. He wished for her to be his hostess and his procuress. He wished for her to be with him in his work, and he always forgave her sweetly. He defended her against the Pharisee who said she was impure and against her sister who said she was idle and against Judas who said she was a waster of goods. When he saw her weep, he could not keep in his own tears, and for her love he raised Lazarus from death to life[6] after he lay dead for four days, and he healed her sister of the flow of blood[7] from which she suffered for seven years.

Because of her merits, he made Marcilla, Martha's handmaid, worthy enough to say these sweet words: "Blessed be the womb that carried you and the breasts that gave you suck." Saint Ambrose says it was Martha who said these words, but they were actually the words of her chambermaid.[8] This Mary, he says, is she who washed the feet of our Lord and wiped them with her hair and anointed them with precious ointments[9] and did solemn penance in the time of grace. She was the first to choose the best part and sat at the feet of our Lord and heard his words.[10] She is the one who anointed his head,[11] was beside the cross at the Passion,[12] readied the ointments, and would have anointed his body and not left that tomb,[13] and she is the one to whom Jesus Christ appeared first when he was resurrected.[14] She was a companion to the apostles who, "after the ascension of our Lord in the fourteenth year of his passion, after the Jews had slain

5 "Mary who is called Magdalen, out of whom seven devils were gone forth" (Luke 8: 2; Mark 16: 2).

6 John 11: 1–45.

7 This malady is commonly called the "bloody flux" or "an issue of blood" and is understood to be an incurable flow of blood, presumably menstrual blood. There are numerous references in the Bible to women being cured of this issue of blood by touching the hem of Christ's garment. Cf. Matt. 9: 20–2, Mark 5: 25, Luke 8: 43 and the occurrence of this malady in *Lucy*.

8 Here the Middle English scribe actively disagrees with Ambrose's account, unless it is a mistranslation from the original Latin.

9 Luke 7: 36–50.

10 This is the "contemplative" Mary who is set against the "busy" Martha; both are used as examples of the ways to serve God, though Mary's service is deemed more pure and more spiritual.

11 Matt. 26: 6–13; Mark 14: 3–9; John 12: 1.

12 Matt. 27: 55–6; Mark 15: 40, 15: 47; Luke 24: 10–11; John 19: 25–7.

13 The two Marys at the sepulchre; Matt. 27: 61.

14 Matt. 28: 1–10; Mark 16: 1–15; John 20: 1–19.

Stephen and driven the other disciples out of that country,"[15] were dispersed abroad among the Gentiles and preached the word of God. At that time, Saint Maximin was among the apostles of the seventy-two disciples of our Lord, to whom Mary Magdalene had been recommended by the blessed Saint Peter. Then the disciples parted ways.

Saint Maxim; Mary Magdalene; Lazarus, her brother; Martha, her sister; Marcilla, Martha's handmaid; and Saint Cenodine, who was born blind but given sight by our Lord[16] – all of these together with many other Christians were taken by the heathens, put into a ship and set adrift on the sea without navigators or sailors, so that they would all be drowned, but, by the will of God, they came to Marseilles.[17] But there they found that no one would receive them into his or her home. So they dwelled on the front porch of a temple of the people of that country. When the blessed Mary Magdalene saw the people assembled at the temple in order to sacrifice to their idols, she arose majestically with a glad visage and a discreet tongue, and speaking well she began to preach the word of Jesus Christ and draw the people from worshiping the idols. Then they marveled greatly at the beauty and reason that was in her and at her fair speech, and it was no wonder that the mouth that so debonairly and so goodly kissed the feet of our Lord was more inspired with the word of God than any other.

After that, it happened that the prince of the province performed a sacrifice to his idols so that he and his wife might have a child. And Mary Magdalene preached about Jesus Christ to him and reproved this sacrifice. After a while, Mary Magdalene appeared to the lady in a vision, saying, "How is it, since you have such great plenty of riches that you dare to leave the poor servants of our Lord to die from hunger, thirst, and cold." The lady was afraid to reveal this to her husband. The second night, Mary Magdalene appeared to her and menaced her greatly, saying that if she would only stir her husband to refresh the poor servants of our Lord, she would absolve her. But the lady would not reveal it to her husband yet. Then on the third night

15 Acts 7: 59; Acts 8: 1–4; description of Stephen's death by stoning, his funeral, and the flight of the apostles, Acts 8: 4: "They therefore that were dispersed went about preaching the word of God."

16 This is probably a reference to the blind man who is given sight in Luke 18: 41–3 or Luke 9.

17 Marseilles; the following material is not biblical but is included in the Digby *Mary Magdalene* play as well as in other apocryphal accounts.

she appeared to them both while they were in bed together and said with an angry countenance: "Do you sleep, you tyrant, limb of your father, Satan, with your wife, the serpent, who does not tell you my words? Rest now, you enemy of the cross, that has a womb full from gluttony. You suffer the saints of God to perish, and you lie in your palace wrapped in clothes of silk. You see them without a house, in discomfort, and you take no heed. You shall not escape so lightly, you felon, nor shall you leave without punishment for abiding so long." When she had said this, she departed, and the lady woke and sighed, and the husband also sighed for the same reason and trembled. And then she said, "Sire, did you see the dream that I saw?" "I have seen it," he said, "and marvel greatly at it and am sorely afraid." Then his wife said to him, "It is more profitable for us to obey her than to run in the wrath of the god about whom she preaches." Because of that they received them into their house and ministered to their needs.

After a while, as Mary Magdalene preached to the aforesaid prince, he said to her, "Do you know how you might defend the law that you preach?" She replied, "Surely, I am ready to defend it as one who is confirmed every day by miracles and by the prediction of our master Saint Peter, who sits in the See of Rome." The prince responded, "I and my wife are ready to obey you in all things if you will, by your prayers, get us a son from the god of whom you preach." Then the Magdalene said, "For that it shall not abide." The blessed Mary Magdalene prayed to our Lord for them that He would, by His mercy, grant them a child, and our Lord heard her prayer and that lady conceived.

Then the husband wanted to go to Saint Peter to prove whether the merits of Jesus Christ were such as Mary preached. Then his wife said to him: "Sire, you wish to go without me? Nay, not for any reason, for when you go, I will go and return, if God wills it, when you return."[18] Her husband replied, "Wife, it may not be so, for you are with child and the perils of the sea are without number and you might easily perish. You shall abide at home and take care of our possessions." The lady protested like a woman and would not change her womanly manners; weeping, she fell down on her knees at his feet. At last, he granted her request. Then Mary Magdalene marked

18 Cf. Ruth 1: 16: "Be not against me, to desire that I should leave thee and depart: for whithersoever thou shalt go, I will go: and where thou shalt dwell, I also will dwell. Thy people shall be my people, and thy God my God." However, Ruth does not say this to her husband but to her mother-in-law, Noemi.

them on their shoulders with the sign of the cross so that the wicked enemy should not put them off their way.

So they charged a ship with a great abundance of goods and all the things that were necessary to them and left all their other possessions in the keeping of Mary Magdalene and went their way. When they had sailed the course of a day and a night, the sea began to swell and the wind increased so that everyone was greatly afraid; namely, the lady who was with child and feeble was full of anguish at such great waves and turbulent seas. Because of her anxiety, the lady suddenly went into labor. Between the great torment of her travail and the strength of time, she brought forth a son and then died. When the child was born, it cried for the breast of its mother and made a piteous noise. Alas, in what sorrow the child was born and made the slayer of his mother, and he must needs die for there was nothing that might nourish him.

Alas, what shall the pilgrim do, who saw his wife dead and his child braying with a weeping voice, seeking the breasts of his mother? The pilgrim wept piteously and said, "Alas, I am wretched, what shall I do? I desired to have a son and now I have lost both the mother and the son." The sailors cried on the other side saying, "We must cast this dead body into the sea, lest we all perish. For as long as it is with us, the tempest will never cease." When they took the body in order to throw it into the sea, the pilgrim said, "Wait awhile, wait, and though you will not spare me my wife, yet spare at least this little babe who weeps and cries. Abide a while to see, by chance, if the woman is in a swoon with woe and pain and may, if God wills it, awake again."

Then a hill appeared not far from the ship, and when he saw it, he thought it better to bear the body and the child there than to cast them into the sea to be devoured by the waves. Then they did so much by prayers and by gifts that they turned their ship toward that hill and bore the bodies to it. When they saw that they could not dig the earth because of the hardness of the rock, they laid her body in the most secret place in the mountain and covered it with a mantle. Then weeping bitterly, the father laid the child at the breast of the mother and said, "Oh Mary Magdalene, you came to Marseilles to my evil fortune. Alas, I am wretched. Why did I take this journey upon me? By your teaching, you have required of your God that my wife should conceive only to perish, her and the child. This is what I have received by your prayers. I recommend her now to you, to whom I have entrusted all my other possessions, and I recommend her to your God. So that if he is powerful, he will help the soul of the mother, and also, by your prayers, he will have pity on the child so that it does not perish." Then he covered all of the mother's body and the child with his mantle and went back to the ship.

When he arrived and approached Saint Peter, Saint Peter challenged him and saw the sign of the cross upon his shoulder. He asked him who he was and from whence he came. He told Peter everything in order. Then Saint Peter said, "Peace be with you. You are welcome for you have believed good counsel.[19] Do not be sorry nor sorrowful, though your wife sleeps and your little son rests with her, for our Lord Jesus Christ is almighty and gives life to whom he will and takes back those he has given when he wishes and can turn all weeping into joy."

Then Saint Peter led him into Jerusalem, and there he showed him all the places where Jesus Christ preached and the places where he suffered death and where he ascended into heaven. When he was well taught in the faith by Saint Peter, two years had passed, so he took his leave of Saint Peter and went to a ship in order to return to his country. As they sailed, they came, by the ordinance of God, near the rock where the bodies of his wife and child had been laid. He did so much by prayers and by gifts that they landed the ship there.

All that time, Mary Magdalene took care of the child, and when he could go, he often went to the seaside. And as the child played with the little stones that he found about the shore, the men arrived, and they found the child playing upon the beach, as was its custom, and they marveled greatly who it might be and approached it. When the child, who had never seen such a thing before, saw them, he was afraid and fled secretly to the bosom of his mother and hid himself under the mantle. Then the pilgrim went to investigate this thing more clearly and saw the beautiful child sucking the breast of his mother. Then he took up the child and said, "Oh blessed Mary Magdalene, how I am blessed; and all things would be well with me if my wife might turn again to life and come with me, home to my country. I know truly and believe without any dread that you have given me the child and have fed him for two years on this rock. Might you also, by your prayers, restore the mother to her first health?" With those words, the mother respired and said, just as though she had woken from a hard sleep, "Blessed Mary Magdalene, you are of

19 Cf. Peter's challenge of Mary's words and ability as a preacher in the Gnostic text "The Gospel According to Mary" in *New Testament Apocrypha*, ed. Edgar Hennecke and Wilhelm Schneemelcher, vol. 1 (London: Lutterworth Press, 1963).

great merit and glorious in the sight of God, for in all the great sorrow of my labor, you were a midwife to me, and in all my necessities, you have benignly served me." When the pilgrim heard this, he marveled to himself and said, "Do you live my true, dear wife?" She replied, "Yes, surely I live and am right now come from the pilgrimage that you came from, and just as the blessed Saint Peter led you about Jerusalem and showed you all the places where our Lord suffered death and was buried and many other places, I was with you, and Mary Magdalene was my companion and my guide. I saw all the places there and have them well in mind." Then all the places and miracles that her husband had seen were embedded in his mind and never left. Then the pilgrim received his wife and child and went joyfully back to the ship.

Within a while after, they arrived at the port of Marseilles and found the blessed Mary Magdalene preaching with her disciples. They kneeled down to her and told her all that had befallen them and received baptism from Saint Maximin. Then they destroyed all the temples of idols in the city of Marseilles and built churches of Jesus Christ and chose, by one accord, the blessed lady to be the bishop of that city.[20] In the end, they came by the will of God to the city of Aix, and by many miracles they brought the people to the faith of God, and Maximin was made bishop there.

In the meantime, the blessed Mary Magdalene was so covetous of the sovereign love of God that she chose a harsh place in the desert to live. She was in that place, which was ordained for her by the hands of angels, for thirty winters without knowledge of any creature; in which place there was no flowing water, nor comfort of trees, nor herbs, so that it could be clearly shown that our Lord would feed her with heavenly meats and not with earthly food.[21] Every day, at every hour of the day, she was lifted up into the air by angels, and she heard their glorious song of heavenly fellowship with bodily ears. Every day she was fed this way with sweet meats, and then she was borne

20 This is a drastic deviation from Ryan, in which Lazarus is elected bishop, not Mary Magadalene (*The Golden Legend*, vol. 1, p. 380). This tradition is not echoed in the Digby Play, and it may have been a scribal error originally. This places Mary Magdalene in a unique position considering her speech usually caused enough anxiety without giving her more overt power. See Alcuin Blamires, "Women and Preaching in Medieval Orthodoxy, Heresy, and Saints' Lives," *Viator* 26 (1995) pp. 135–52.

21 This section of *Mary Magdalene* is reminiscent of *Mary of Egypt* and is an example of how the figure of Mary Magdalene was formed from different sources, creating a composite saint.

by these angels back to her proper place so that she had no need of bodily nourishment.

So it happened in time that a priest who desired to live a solitary life took a cell for himself only twelve bowshots from her place. One day, our Lord opened the eyes of that priest, who saw with his bodily eyes the way the angels descended to the place where Mary Magdalene dwelled and how they lifted her up in the air and then afterwards, in the space of an hour, how they brought her back again to the same place with divine praise. Then the priest desired to know the truth of that marvelous vision and recommended himself, by his prayers, to our Lord, his maker, and went surely with great devotion to that place. When he drew near by a stone's throw, his thighs began to grow stiff as though they were tightly bound, and all his insides began to tremble from fear. When he turned to leave, his thighs and his feet were ready to go, but when he forced himself to go to that place, his whole body was languid and would not move. Then he understood without fail that it was a secret, heavenly thing and place that no earthly man could reach. Then he called the name of Jesus Christ and cried, "I conjure you, by the virtue of our Lord, if you be man or any other reasonable creature that dwells in that pit, you answer me and tell me the truth of yourself."

When he had said this three times, the blessed Mary Magdalene answered and said, "Come nearer and you shall know the truth of your desire." He came trembling halfway toward her, and then she said to him, "Have you knowledge of the Gospel that makes mention of that rightly named sinful woman who wet and washed the feet of Our Savior with her tears and wiped them with her hair and deserved forgiveness for her sins?"[22] The priest replied, "I remember well, lady, and it is more than thirty winters since the Church believes and confesses it was done." Then she said, "It is I, who by the space of thirty winters have been here without any worldly fellowship and as you were allowed to see yesterday. Just like that I am lifted up into the air every day by the hands of angels and have deserved to hear with my mortal ears seven times each day the sweet song of the heavenly fellowship. Because it has been shown to me that I shall pass out of this world, go to Saint Maximin and tell him that the day after the Resurrection of our Lord, at the same time that he usually goes to matins, he should enter his oratory alone and there he shall find me by the mystery and service of angels."

22 Luke 7:36–50.

The priest heard her voice, like the voice of an angel, but he saw nothing. Then he went straightway to Saint Maximin and told him everything in order. Maximin was filled with great joy and gave great thanks to our Lord. On the day and hour it was told to him, he entered into his oratory and saw the blessed Mary Magdalene, who was in the choir in the fellowship of angels who had brought her there. She was lifted up from the earth two cubits in height and prayed, holding her hands straight up to our Lord. Saint Maximin was afraid to go to her. She turned toward him and said, "Come hither, my own father, and flee not your daughter." When he neared her, as it is read in the works of Saint Maximin, he saw that because of the continual vision of angels every day, the visage of this holy lady shone as though it were a bright beam of the sun. Then all the priests were called and blessed Mary received the body of our Lord from the bishop with a great abundance of tears. After that, she stretched her body before the altar and her holy soul passed to our Lord. After the passing of her holy spirit, so great a savor of sweetness abode there that it was felt among them for the space of seven days. Saint Maximin anointed her body with diverse ointments, and buried her worshipfully, and he has since ordained that he is to be buried with her after his death.

Egypsus, according to some books, and Josephus agree well with this story, because Josephus says, in a tract that he wrote, that Mary Magdalene, after the ascension of our Lord, was so set afire with the charity of Jesus Christ that because of the sorrow and annoyance she felt, she would see no man. Therefore, when she came to the land of Aix, she went into the desert and dwelled there for thirty years without knowledge of any creature. And he describes how canonically every day, in every hour, she was lifted up into the air by angels. But he says that when the priest came to her, he found her closed in her cell, and she asked him for a cloth. He took her one, and then she went with him to the church, and there she received her communion and then went to her prayers, her hands joined to our Lord, and so rested in peace.

In the time of Charlemagne, in the year of our Lord 769, the duke of Burgundy[23] could not have a child with his wife; wherefore he gave his goods largely to the poor people and founded many churches. When he built the Abbey of Vezelay,[24] he and the abbot of

23 Gerard, duke of Burgundy.

24 This legend is later changed by the Dominicans after 1458, who claimed that

that church sent a monk with sufficient surety to Aix in order to bring from there, if he could, the relics of Mary Magdalene. This monk came to this city and found it completely destroyed by the pagans, but by chance he found the marble sarcophagus that showed that the blessed body of Mary Magdalene rested within it, and her story was marvelously inscribed upon it. Then the monk opened it by night, took the relics, and bore them with him to his house. That same night, Mary Magdalene appeared to him saying, "Do not dread, but perform your work." When he was half a mile from his monastery, he could not in any way move the relics further until the abbot and the monks came in procession and received them worshipfully.

A knight, who by custom visited the body of Mary Magdalene every year, was slain in battle. As his friends wept for him on his bier, they said in a sweet complaining manner to Mary Magdalene, "Ah, good lady, why have you suffered your devout servant to die without shrift and penance?" Then he who was dead arose suddenly before them all and called for a priest, who shrove him with great devotion, and he received the Sacrament, and then rested in peace.

There was a ship that sank, filled with men and women who were drowning in the sea, and among them there was a woman with child who was also drowning. As much as she might, in her mind she called Mary Magdalene, begging her to help her escape through her merits, and she promised that if she had a son she would yield him to the church. As soon as she made this vow, a woman of great beauty in worshipful clothing appeared to her, took her by the chin, brought her to land completely whole, and all the others perished. After that, she brought forth a son and fulfilled her vow well.

Some say that Mary Magdalene was wedded to Saint John the Evangelist[25] and that our Lord called him from the wedding and she, out of spite because our Lord had taken away her husband, gave her body to all the delights of the flesh. But because it was not acceptable that the calling of Saint John should be the occasion of her temptation and damnation, our Lord converted her piteously to penance,

Mary's relics were buried in the Church of Saint Maximin in Aix-en-Provence. The *Dominican Legend* was written to emphasize the connection between the Angevin House, the Dominican Order of Preachers, and Mary Magdalene (Jansen, *The Making of the Magdalen*, pp. 43–4).

25 According to Jacobus, this part of *Mary Magdalene* is discussed by "Brother Albert in his intro to the Gospel of Saint John." Ryan says this is most likely Saint Albert the Great (OP), an older contemporary of Jacobus. However, this attribution has been left out of this version of *Mary Magdalene*.

and because of that he took her from fleshly delight and filled her with sovereign, heavenly delight that was his own love. They say that she worshiped him before others with the sweetness of his familiarity, in as much as he had taken her from her earlier delight.

A man who was blind had himself led to the church of Mary Magdalene by way of a pilgrimage to visit her shrine. As they walked, his guide said to him that he saw the church, and then the blind man cried with a high voice and said, "Ah, blessed Mary Magdalene that I might deserve, in time, to see your church." And anon, his eyes were opened and he saw clearly.

A man wrote his sins on a scroll and laid it under the altar, praying for Mary Magdalene in her goodness to ask for grace for him. And with that, in a while, he took the scroll and found all his sins erased.

There was a man who was held in prison for debt, and he called to his aid the blessed Mary Magdalene many times. One night there appeared to him a fair woman who broke his irons, undid his door, and bade him go fast on his way, and when he felt himself unbound, he quickly fled.

A clerk of Flanders, who was called Steven, fell into such great wretchedness that he haunted all kinds of sins, and that which belonged to his spiritual health he would not hear. Notwithstanding that, he always had great devotion to Mary Magdalene, fasted, and worshiped her feast. One time he visited her tomb between sleeping and waking, and when he woke, Mary Magdalene appeared to him in the likeness of a fair woman supported by two angels on each side. She said to him with a despiteful look, "Steven, why do you account the deeds of my merits so unworthy? Why are you not, by the instance of my merits, moved to repentance? Since you began to have devotion for me, I have always steadfastly prayed for you, and therefore, rise up and repent, and I will not leave you until you are reconciled with God." With that, he felt such a great deal of grace coming into him that he forsook the world and entered into religion and led a true, perfect life. At his death, Mary Magdalene was said to stand beside his bier with angels and bear his soul with her in the form of a dove. Here ends the life of the blessed Mary Magdalene.

Saint Thais, Courtesan

The life of Saint Thais serves a two-fold purpose: she represents the repentant sinners, but she also serves as an early example of the anchorite tradition, which was flourishing in the thirteenth century when Jacobus compiled his text. Her life, which Jacobus says is taken from *The Life of the Fathers* by Saint Ambrose, may seem unusually harsh and strict to modern audiences, but her form of penance would not have been alien or abhorrent to a medieval audience. The tradition of walling women up in cells to voluntarily become "anchors" of the church, both literally and figuratively, was not uncommon. Like many medieval recluses and anchorites, including Julian of Norwich, Thais is shut away to dwell on her sins and serve her repentance in contemplation. Thais, as a Christian courtesan, knows her sin and responds willingly to Abbot Payne's offer of repentance that she receives by being enclosed in a cell for three years. After the time has passed, Payne remembers her and seeks advice from Abbot Anthony, who is most likely the Saint Anthony who retreated into the desert to seek solitude himself, faced a number of temptations, gained a multitude of disciples, and then retreated into solitude once more. Anthony has his disciple Paul, who is probably Saint Paul, the first hermit, pray for a sign of her forgiveness. The vision is revealed and she is released only to die in peace within two weeks. Her story may have served as a model for later medieval recluses who were generally confined for life in small cells attached to churches. While a harsh and seemingly brutal punishment, it is deemed appropriate for Thais: "As if the enclosure and the rigorous program of prayer were not enough, privation and pain through fasting, vigils, the wearing of uncomfortable clothing and flagellation would be embraced. Total sexual abstinence was required."[1] This is an appropriate punishment for a whore who knowingly and willingly commits sins of the flesh. She accepts her punishment quietly without protest, a distinction that is drawn between her and the courtesan at the end of the text, who is not

1 Hugh White, introduction to *Ancrene Wisse: Guide for Anchoresses* (London: Penguin Books, 1993) p. viii.

converted by the revelation of her sin by Abbot Ephram. She must be a willing participant in order to be saved; no one can do it for her. Her punishment and the later medieval texts concerning the practices of recluses and anchoresses, such as the thirteenth-century *Ancrene Wisse*, serve as a sharp reminder of the validity of the ascetic principle for many early Christians.[2] However, Thais' account deviates from *Ancrene Wisse*, which actively discourages flagellation and wearing hair-shirts for penance, and does not envision sanitation arrangements that require the anchorite to sit in her own waste to contemplate her sins. Thais is forgotten during her confinement and dies after her release, just as later anchoresses were treated as dead. The anchorhold was intended to be a tomb; the anchorites were essentially buried alive, embracing this symbolic death as following the teachings of Christ.[3] This was not an uncommon phenomenon; there is evidence of 780 anchorites on some 600 sites in England between 1100 and 1539.[4] The reclusive life fulfilled the demands of self-denial and suffering and is used to illustrate how drastic Thais' transformation really is. Her symbolic death as she is walled up in her cell signifies the death of her wicked ways and her previous lifestyle. She is reborn into the world after her penance, but leaves it for a heavenly reward. Parallels came be drawn between Thais' life and those of the holy transvestites who enclose themselves not only in a monastery but also in the male identity. Thais has no identity; she ceases to exist once the mortar is in place and is only remembered to prove her redemption to her witnesses. Unlike Mary Magdalene, her voice is quiet and unchallenging, yet we see wisdom in her words. She is aware of her position and accepts the opportunity for salvation that is presented to her. Unlike the holy transvestites, her silence becomes her form of expression because, as mentioned earlier, not every common woman is as open to redemption as Thais, and not every holy man can bring it about. This episode takes the responsibility out of Payne's hands and places it firmly in hers.

2 White, introduction to *Ancrene Wisse*, p. ix.

3 Cf. John 12: 25: "he who loves his life loses it, and he who hates his life in this world will keep it for eternal life."

4 White, Introduction to *Ancrene Wisse*, p. xiv. Also see Ann Warren, *Anchorites and Their Patrons in Medieval England* (Berkeley: University of California Press, 1985) and Christopher Holdsworth, "Hermits and the Power of the Frontier," *Reading Medieval Studies* 16 (1990) pp. 55–76, for a discussion on the social function of anchorites and recluses.

The Life of Saint Thais, Courtesan

Thais, as it is read in *The Life of the Fathers*, was a common woman of such great beauty that many followed her, sold all their sustenance, and fell into poverty. Those who loved her fought each other many times out of jealousy and often slew each other, so that because of their fighting her house was full of blood and the young men who were drawn to her.

So in time, a holy man named Payne heard of her wretchedness. Dressing in secular clothing, he took a shilling and went into an Egyptian city. He gave her this shilling, that is twelve ducats, in order to commit a sin. When she had taken this money, she said to him, "We shall go into the chamber together." When they were in the room, she bade him to get in the bed that was richly covered with a sumptuous blanket. Then he said to her, "Is there not a more secret place here where we can go?" She led him to diverse places in the house, but he always said that he was afraid of being seen. "There is a place," she said, "that no man visits, and no man shall know what we do except God." Then he said to her, "You know God exists and sees all things clearly?" She replied, "I believe in God and that he sees and knows all things quite clearly." Then that blessed man said, "You say you know all this, but do you not know how he will punish sinners with endless torments of hell and reward those who live virtuously with sovereign bliss in heaven?" She said, "All this I know and believe." He replied, "If you know all this, why have you ruined so many souls? Understand that not only will you be damned for your own sins, but you will have to account, by pain, for all those you have brought to sin."

When she heard this she kneeled down at Abbot Payne's[5] feet, and with bitter tears begged him to receive her penance. She said, "Father, I understand well what penance is, and I know well that by my prayers I may have forgiveness. I only ask for the space of three hours, and after that I will go wherever you want me to, and do and obey whatever you command." When he had agreed to grant her time and assigned a place where she should meet him, she went and gathered together all her things that she had received in sin, bore them all to the middle of the city before all the people, and burned them in a

5 Abba. Paphnutius in Ryan. William Granger Ryan, *The Golden Legend: Readings on the Saints* (Princeton: Princeton University Press, 1993) vol. 2, p. 235.

bonfire saying, "Come hither to me, all of you who have sinned with me, and see how I burn everything that you have given me." The value of the gold and the rings was five hundred pounds.

When she had burned everything, she went to the place assigned by Abbot Payne; it was a church of virgins where he enclosed her in a cell and sealed the door with lead. The cell was small and close, and they left only a little window by which they could minister to her needs. The abbot commanded that every day they should give her a little bread and a little water. As the abbot turned to go, Thais said, "Father, where do you command that I put my natural waste?" He replied, "In the cell as you deserve." Then she asked how she should pray to God, and he replied, "You are not worthy to utter the name of God or the Trinity, nor to lift up your hands to heaven, for your lips have been full of wickedness and your hands have wickedly touched filth. So look only toward the east and repeat these words: 'Lord who created me, have mercy and pity on me.' "

When she had been enclosed in this pit for three years, the abbot remembered her and thought of her. Then he went to Abbot Anthony[6] to inquire whether God had forgiven her sins and related her story to him. Saint Anthony then called his disciples and commanded them to stay awake that night and pray that God would, in his mercy, declare the cause of Abbot Payne's visit. As they prayed without ceasing, the Abbot Paul, who was the greatest of Anthony's disciples, suddenly saw a bed in heaven arrayed with precious clothes tended by three virgins with clear faces. The three virgins were, firstly, the dread of the pains of hell that drew Thais away from her sins; secondly, the shame for the sins she had committed; and thirdly, the love of righteousness that lifted her up to the sovereign place and made her deserve pardon. When Paul said that the grace of that vision was due only to the merits of Saint Anthony, a heavenly voice was heard saying that it was not by the merits of Anthony but by the merits of Thais, the sinful woman.

In the morning, when Abbot Paul described this vision and they all knew the will of God, Abbot Payne departed with great joy, went

6 Most likely Saint Anthony of Egypt, who was also a hermit and a recluse in the desert, despite having a number of disciples, and a contemporary of Saint Paul, the first hermit who is named here as "the greatest of Anthony's disciples." It is fitting that Saint Anthony is part of her legend because of the temptation he was subjected to during his time in the desert, including visions of naked women and a richly attired courtesan. He resisted those temptations, and in this legend he is seen as an instrument of Thais' redemption.

to the monastery where she was kept, and opened the door of the cell. She asked if she could stay longer, but the abbot said, "Come out, for your sins have been forgiven by God." She answered, "I take God as my witness that, since I entered this cell, I set all my sins before my eyes. And just as the breath never parts from the mouth or nostrils, my sins never left my sight. I have always beheld them and wept for them." The abbot replied, "Then God has forgiven your sins not only because of your penance but also because you have always had fear in your courage." He took her out of there, and she lived fifteen days afterward before resting in peace with our Lord.

The Abbot Ephram wanted to convert a common woman in the same way. As that wretched woman drew Saint Ephram foolishly into sin, he said to her, "Follow me," and she followed him. When they came to a crowded place he said to her, "Sit down for I will have sex with you here." She replied, "How can I commit such a sin in front of such a multitude of people?" He answered, "If you have shame in front of men, how much greater is your shame in front of God, the Creator, who knows all things?" Then she left completely confused.[7] Here ends the life of Saint Thais.

7 This example highlights how Thais is saved through her own merits and hidden virtues and not necessarily through the efforts of Abbot Payne. She already knew what sin was and believed in it; he just reminded her of the penalty and gave her a means by which she could repent.

Saint Marina

In addition to belonging to the corpus of Jacobus's *Golden Legend*, the life of Saint Marina appears to have its source in local tradition. According to *Butler's Lives of Saints*, "The story of this Marina is simply one of those popular romances of women masquerading as men."[1] Another Middle English version of this story is found in the *Northern Homily Cycle*, which is an adaptation of the story found in AN *Vitas Patrum*.[2] The prose version translated here is also found in the *Legende Doree* and Christine de Pizan's *The Book of the City of Ladies*. While widely disseminated during the medieval period, very little has been written recently on the English versions of these "holy transvestites." However, Marina's legend is one of five transvestite legends in the *Gilte Legende*, three of which, including *Marina,* follow the same pattern: a woman who lives as a man is falsely accused of impregnating a local girl, accepts the crime and the punishment, and is only vindicated after her death when her true gender is discovered.

As discussed in the introduction, Marina's life is unique because she is more genderless than her counterparts; she is disguised as a boy early in her life by her own father. For her, the gender transformation is not a conscious choice that she makes herself, just as the discovery of her true gender is not her choice. She lives as a man to avoid detection and the possibility of expulsion from the only life she knows, as well as the very real threat of sexual assault. She knows she is a woman but does not necessarily know what that distinction entails. Therefore, as Susanna Fein points out, "Her cross-dressed state maintains, nonetheless, her unspotted record of purity. The unknowing monks did *not* desire her. Her woman's body could *not* have raped the dairyman's daughter. She herself could not have

1 Alban Butler, *Butler's Lives of Saints* (New York: P. J. Kennedy and Sons, 1963).

2 Susanna Fein, "A Saint 'Geynest under Gore': Marina and the Love Lyrics of the Seventh Quire" in *Studies in the Harley Manuscript: The Scribes, Contents, and Scribal Contexts of British Library MS Harley 2253* (Kalamazoo, Mich.: Medieval Institute Publications, 2000) p. 360 n. 25.

comprehended what actions lay behind the accusation."[3] While Marina remains steadfastly silent through the accusation and her subsequent punishment, her body speaks for her when she dies; it becomes the voice and the spectacle of her purity and her innocence, while providing a titillating glimpse at the forbidden for all the monks who crowd in to witness this miracle. In the verse version of *Marina* that is the subject of Fein's article, this presents a number of other issues causing the tale to look "suspiciously profane in motive."[4] However, Fein discusses the version of *Marina* found among love lyrics in British Library MS Harley 2253, lyrics that follow a thread of profanity and objectification that encompasses the saint's life. The prose *Marina* is not troubled by this context, and indeed, the language of the *Gilte Legende* version varies significantly from that found in Harley MS 2253. However, the gender issues are still prevalent and shape the voice of this tender, guileless saint.

The Life of Saint Marina

Saint Marina was a noble virgin and an only child, alone with her father, without brothers and sisters. Her father, after the death of her mother, entered into a monastery of monks and changed the clothing of his daughter so that men would think she was his son. Then the father begged the abbot of the house and the monks to receive his son as a monk, for he had no other children. They accepted him gladly, and among them he was called Brother Marinus.

Marina lived very religiously and was obedient in all things. When she was twenty-seven years old, her father felt that he was sick and near to death. He called his daughter to him and reaffirmed her in her good purpose, and he charged her, upon his blessing, that she should never reveal to any creature that she was a woman. And so he died. She abode in her holy purpose and continued her life as a holy monk, unknown to all creatures that she was a woman.

She often went with other monks to the woods with their cart and their oxen to bring wood back to their monastery. Their custom when they went out like this was to harbor themselves in the house of a franklin who had a daughter, who conceived a child by a knight.

3 Fein, "A Saint 'Geynest under Gore'," p. 363.
4 Fein, "A Saint 'Geynest under Gore'," p. 365.

When it was perceived, and she realized who the father was, she declared firmly that it was the monk Marinus who had gotten her with child. When her father and mother heard this, they went to the abbot and raised a horrible clamor upon him for his monk. The abbot, having great shame and sorrow because of this foul clamor, sent for Marinus and asked him why he had committed such a horrible sin. He answered meekly and said, "Holy father, I ask our Lord mercy for I have sinned." The abbot, hearing this, was out of himself for sorrow and shame and commanded that Marinus should shamefully be put out of their monastery.

He patiently lived outside and dwelled continuously at the gate for three years, during which they threw him a morsel of bread a day. When the child was born, it was sent to the abbot, and he sent it immediately to Marinus[5] and bade him to keep such treasure as he had brought forth. Then this saintly Marinus meekly and patiently took his child, kissed it, wept hard, and kept it tenderly in his power and patiently thanked the God of all. She kept the child two years, and at last her brethren had great pity and compassion for her humility and for her patience, and prayed to the abbot to have pity on him. Her brethren, considering the great punishment and shame that he had received, and also the great meekness and obedience that they saw in him, beseeched the abbot, in reverence of God, to forgive him and receive him into their monastery again. So, at last, the abbot with great insistence granted this, charging that he should be assigned to all the foul occupations that were done in that monastery. He meekly and patiently did all these services gladly and devoutly, and thus endured his life in holy works until she passed to our Lord.

The brethren then went to the abbot to ask where they should bring the body. He answered and said in the wildest place that they could find outside the cemetery – saying that Marinus had defiled himself so horribly that he should not be among his brethren in any holy place. Then they went to wash this body, as was the custom, and as they washed her, they discovered that she was a woman. In that sight they were hugely abashed and ran in great haste after the abbot, saying to him, "Father, come, come and see the marvels of God." Marveling greatly at what they meant, he went with them. When he

5 This is the masculine form of Marina and is used with the male pronoun to indicate the shift in gender, according to the disguise of the female saint in male attire and the perception of the monks around her. The scribe switches his use of gender pronouns just as the reader's perception of Marina's gender changes.

saw that she was a woman, he fell down to the ground asking mercy and grace for the injury he had done to her, imploring her to take no vengeance upon him for his ignorance and misdeed, saying to the body with great weeping and sighing: "Ah, holy chambermaid of our Lord, what wrongs have I done to teach a holy, pure virgin. Forgive me, for I have too sorely offended God and thee. You say in your great meekness 'Father, I have sinned.'[6] But I may say, because of my great wickedness, 'mother and sister.'[7] I have grievously sinned to God and thee and said in my malice that you should be buried in a vile place. But holy virgin, you have deserved a precious place of cleanliness. Therefore you shall lie in the most worshipful place in our monastery, for you are our worship and our joy." Thus, with great sorrow and lamentation, they washed the body and took it up and bore it with great reverence to the church. With that, the bells of the monastery began to ring solemnly by themselves, and so they continued until this blessed body was buried.

The woman who defamed this holy Marina was vexed by a demon, confessed her felony, came to the sepulchre of this virgin, and was healed. All the people assembled around her tomb and praised God for his virgin. Many notable miracles were done there continually. She passed to our Lord the fourteenth day of July. Here ends the life of Saint Marina.

6 In the text it is "Pater peccavi."
7 In the text, "Mater et soror."

Saint Theodora

Jacobus does not list a source for this legend, but Theodora is another example of a holy transvestite. While her story shares some similarities with that of Marina, the basis of it is completely different. Theodora is a sinner; she commits adultery and then takes the habit of a monk to repent her sin. Unlike Marina, who is pure and ignorant of the difference between the sexes, Theodora knowingly hides all vestiges of her gender to erase all trace of her crime. The scribe reflects this by changing the gender of the personal pronoun he uses in reference to her according to whom she is dealing with and their perception of her as either a man or a woman. The gender switch has further implications than mere semantics. Theodora seeks advice from an abbess who tells her that she has indeed committed a sin, but she does not seek refuge in the convent among the nuns. She must completely disavow her sex. It is an interesting dichotomy compared to the open defiance of Saint Eugenia and the meek ignorance of Marina. Theodora never protests, nor does she reveal herself; she lives falsely accused as a man instead of guilty as a woman. The irony rests in the revelation of her true sex after her death; the gender that was the instigation of her sin becomes the instrument of her salvation.

The Life of Saint Theodora

Theodora was a fair noble woman from Alexandria during the reign of Emperor Zeno. She was married to a rich man and lived in dread of God. Satan envied her holiness and inspired a rich man to fall in love with her, pester her greatly with gifts and messages, and insist that she consent to his desires. But she refused the messages and despised the gifts. He continued to bother her busily so that she had no respite and was almost overcome. After all that, he sent an enchanter to her, who begged her to have pity on that man and consent to him. When she told him that she would not commit such a great sin in the sight of God, he enjoined her with words saying, "I know well that God knows and sees whatever is done by day. But when it is evening and the sun has gone down, God sees nothing that is done." Then Theodora said to the enchanter, "You do not speak the truth." He answered slyly, "I speak the truth." Theodora was deceived by the words of the enchanter and told him that when it was evening he should tell his master to come to her and she would fulfill his desire. When he told this to the man, he was filled with great joy. He came at the assigned hour, lay with her, and then went his way.

When Theodora came to her senses, she wept bitterly and beat her face, wailing, "Alas for me, alas for me because I have lost my soul and destroyed the beauty of my name." Her husband came in from outside and saw his wife so discomfited and weeping but did not know the cause. He tried to comfort her, but she would not be comforted. The next day she went to a convent and asked the abbess if God could know a sin done by night. The abbess told her that nothing could be hidden from God because he sees and knows all that is done, regardless of the hour. Theodora wept bitterly saying, "Give me the book of the Gospel so that I may choose my lot." She opened the book and found written within, "What is written is written."[1] She went back to her house; then, when her husband was out, she donned the clothing of a man and went to the monastery that was seven miles away and asked to be received by the monks. They took her in and asked her name; she replied that it was Theodore.

She humbly did all the offices of the order and her service was agreeable to all. Within a year, the abbot bade him[2] to couple the oxen, go to town, and bring them oil. During that time her husband greatly dreaded that she had gone away with some other man. The angel of our Lord said to him, "Rise early in the morning tomorrow and stand in the road of Martyrs Peter and Paul, and she whom you meet there is your wife." Theodora came along the road then with the camels, saw her husband, recognized him, and said to herself, "Alas, my good husband, how I struggle to bring myself out of the sin I committed against you." When he neared her, she greeted him and said "our Lord give you joy, my lord." But he did not recognize her, and after he had waited there a long while he felt that he had been

1 The Latin text reads: "Respondit Pilatus: Quod scripsi scripsi," which is a quotation from John 19: 22: "Pilate said: What I have written, I have written."

2 This is the first place where the gender of the pronoun switches according to the perception of the audience and the monks with whom Theodora is living.

deceived. A voice said to him, "The same person who saluted you this morning was your wife."

Saint Theodora was of such great holiness that she performed many miracles: she rescued a man from wild beasts; he was torn to pieces but she raised him from death to life by her prayers, and she followed that beast, cursed it, and immediately it fell dead. The devil envied her holiness so much that he could not tolerate her. He appeared to her, saying, "You wicked woman and adulteress, you have left your husband in order to come here and spite me. Because of my dreadful virtues, I shall raise such a battle against you that if I do not make you reject your crucified one, then do not call me Satan." She made the sign of the cross and he vanished away.

One time as she came from town with the camels and took shelter in a hostel, a maid came to him and said, "Sleep with me tonight." When he refused her, she went and lay with another man who got her with child. When her belly rose, they asked her who had gotten her with child, and she said it was the monk Theodore who had lain with her. When the child was born, her parents sent it to the abbot of Theodore's monastery. The abbot greatly blamed Theodora, and she prayed meekly for forgiveness. The abbot took the child to her, shoved her out of the gates, and bade her keep with sorrow that which she had gotten in such great sin and shame.

For seven years she nourished that child with the milk of beasts. The fiend envied her patience, so he transfigured himself into the likeness of her husband and said to her: "What are you doing here my wife? I languish for you and have no comfort. Come with me, you who are all my joy. For even though you have lain with another man, I shall forgive you for it." She believed that he was her husband and replied, "I can no longer be with you because the son of Sir John, the knight, has lain with me, and I will do my penance because I have sinned against you." Then she began to pray. The fiend vanished away and she recognized that it was truly the devil.

Another time, the devil tried to scare her by coming to her in the likeness of three wild beasts. A man said to them, "Eat this wicked woman." Then she prayed and they vanished away. Another time, a great multitude of knights came to her. Their prince came forward and each of them worshiped her. Then one of the knights said to her, "Theodora rise up and worship our prince." She replied, "I only worship God Almighty." When they repeated this to their prince, he commanded that she be brought forth and tortured so greatly that men would deem her dead, and then all that company vanished away. Yet another time, she came there and found a great heap of gold. She blessed herself, commended herself to God, and fled away. Another time, she saw a pannier full of all kinds of diverse meats carried by a man who said, "Our prince who beat you sent you this and bade you take it and eat it, because you sinned unknowingly." She blessed herself and he vanished away.

After the seven years had passed, the abbot considered the patience of that brother, reconciled with him, and let him back in the monastery with his brethren along with his son. When she had fulfilled her responsibilities admirably for two years, she took her child and closed him with her in her cell. When the abbot was told of this, he sent some of his monks secretly to find out what she would say to him. She took the child, held him, and kissed him, saying, "My right dear son, the time of my life has come to an end, and therefore I leave you to God so that he may be your father and your helper. Son, make sure you abide in fasting and in worship, and serve your brethren devoutly." In saying that, she yielded up the spirit and slept in our Lord about the year of our Lord AD 470. When the child saw this, he began to weep grievously.

That night, the abbot was shown a vision: he thought he saw a great wedding ordained; all the orders of angels, prophets, martyrs, and saints were there. In the middle of them, there was a woman beset with such great joy that nothing could describe it, and she came right to the wedding and set herself upon the bed. All those who were about her did her worship; then a voice said to the abbot: "This is Theodora who was falsely accused of begetting the child. The times have changed for her, because she has been chastised for defiling the bed of her husband." Then the abbot awoke greatly moved and went to her cell with his brethren, and found her dead. Then he entered into the cell, uncovered her, and found out she was a woman.

The abbot sent for the father of the woman who defamed Theodora and said to him, "Lo, the man whom your daughter defamed is dead." They took away the cloth and saw that she was a woman. All those who saw or heard this thing had great dread. Then the angel of our Lord spoke to the abbot and said, "Arise hastily and get upon your horse. Ride into the city, and if you meet anyone take him and bring him here." As the abbot went forth, he met a man running in his direction, and the abbot asked him where he was going. He answered, "I go to see my wife who is dead." Then the abbot took Theodora's husband upon his horse and brought him to the monastery, and there he wept greatly. They buried the body with great devotion. Then Theodora's husband took his wife's cell, dwelled there, and at his death slept in our Lord. The child of

Theodora followed his nurse in all virtues and works, and increased so greatly in the name of goodness that, when the abbot was dead, he was chosen over all to be the abbot. Here ends the life of Saint Theodora.

Saint Pelagia

As a transvestite saint, Pelagia is not terribly remarkable; she is a sinful woman, converted to Christianity, who dresses as a man, and takes the cell of a hermit. However, there are aspects of her legend that are intriguing to a modern reader. As a repentant sinner and a holy transvestite, Pelagia fits neatly into both categories. Her repentance is marked by her adoption of male clothing, though she is not being punished like Thais, nor is she falsely accused like Marina, Theodora, and Margaret Pelagia. She voluntarily takes on the habit of a male hermit to hide from the world; she is rendered unrecognizable by the extremity of her penance and the severity of her life. She does not reveal herself but is discovered, like many of her compatriots, after her death. However, since she has committed no crime, real or imagined, while in her disguise, the discovery of her true gender lacks the quality of vindication. She appears more as a composite saint: perhaps a combination of Margaret Pelagia and Saint Thais. Jacobus does not name a source for this legend, and it may be one from local tradition that was adapted into the *Legenda Aurea* and later into the *Gilte Legende*.

The Life of Saint Pelagia

Pelagia was the worthiest of the city of Antioch and possessed many riches and worldly goods. She had a beautiful body and noble clothes, but she was vain, had variable courage, and was unchaste. Once, as she went through the town in her great splendor, nothing could be seen on her but gold, silver, and precious stones. Wherever she went she filled the air with the flavor of sweet savors, and a great multitude of young men and women richly and nobly clothed went before her.

A holy bishop called Noyron, bishop of Leopolois,[1] that is now

1 Veronus, bishop of Heliopolis, in Ryan. William Granger Ryan, *The Golden Legend: Readings on the Saints* (Princeton: Princeton University Press, 1993) vol. 2, p. 231.

called Damietta, passed by the city and saw her. He began to weep bitterly because she had more care and business in pleasing the world then he had in pleasing God. He fell down on the pavement and beat his face on the earth, wetting the ground with his tears. He cried on high saying, "Lord have mercy on me, sinful because the great care and business of one sinful woman's array has surpassed all the wisdom of my life. Good Lord, do not let the attire of this wretched woman confound me before the sight of your dreadful majesty. She has arrayed herself with all her power in order to please earthly things, and I have purposed to please the endless God, which in my negligence I have not fulfilled." Then he said to those who were with him, "I tell you in truth that God will bring this woman in judgment against us, for as much as she does great harm in painting herself in order to please worldly lovers, we are guilty of sloth in pleasing the heavenly spouse."

As he said these things and many others, he suddenly fell asleep, and dreamed that he was at Mass, and a black dove, totally befouled, flew busily about him and commanded that all those who were not baptized would be void, and anon the dove disappeared. After Mass she reappeared and the same bishop plunged her into a vessel of water so that she came out white and clean, and flew so high that she could not be seen. Then he awoke, and in a while when he went to the church to preach, Pelagia was present. Through the goodness and mercy of God, she had such great compunction that she sent the bishop letters saying, "Holy bishop, servant of God and true disciple, I am Pelagia, the disciple of the fiend. If you are a proven, true disciple of Christ who, as I have heard told, came down from heaven for sinners, vouchsafe to receive me, sinful repentant." To whom he sent a reply, saying, "I pray you not to despise my humbleness, for I am a sinful man, but if you desire to be saved, you may not see me alone, you may only see me among others." When she came to him before a crowd of people, she fell down at his feet, wept bitterly, and said, "I am Pelagia, mother of wickedness, the flood of sins, the depth of perdition. I am the devourer of souls. I have deceived many whom I now loathe." Then the bishop asked her name and she answered, "At my birth I was called Pelagia, but because of the pomp and pride of my array, men call me Margaret."[2] Then the bishop received her benignly, enjoined her penance, taught her diligently in

2 Ryan's translation adds the definition of "marguerite" as "pearl": ". . . the Pearl, for the preciousness of my attire" (*The Golden Legend*, vol. 2, p. 231).

the laws of God, and baptized her with the Holy Sacrament. The fiend who was present said, "Oh what violence I suffer from this old crooked fellow. Oh you violence, oh you wicked one, cursed be the day when you were born contrary to me, for you have taken my greatest hope from me!"[3]

One night, as Pelagia slept, the fiend came to her and said, "Oh Lady Margaret, what harm have I ever done to you? Have I not arrayed you with all kinds of riches and glory? I pray you, tell me how I have displeased you and I shall swiftly make amends. But however it is, I beseech you not to forsake me lest I be reproved by Christian men." Then she made the sign of the cross, blew upon him, and he suddenly vanished away.

The third day after this, she gathered everything she had together and distributed it among poor men. After a while, unknown to anyone, she stole away by night, went to Mount Olivet, and took the habit of a hermit. She closed herself in a little cell and served God in great abstinence. She was held in great fame by all the people, and she was called Brother Pelagian. After that, a deacon of the bishop who had christened her went to Jerusalem to visit that holy place. The bishop said to him, "When you have visited the holy places, go and visit a holy monk named Pelagian, who is the true servant of God."

When he got there, she recognized him, but he did not know her because she was disfigured by penance. Pelagian said, "You have a bishop?" And he said, "Yes." Then she said, "Ask him to pray for me, for surely he is a true apostle of Jesus Christ." Then he went his way. The third day he came back and knocked at her door, but there was no answer. He went and opened a window and saw her dead. He ran to the bishop and told him. At once, the bishop and his clerks assembled together with all the monks to perform a service for that holy man. When they brought the body out of the cell, they discovered that she was a woman. They all marveled greatly, gave thanks to God, and buried her body worshipfully. She died the eighth day of October in the year of our Lord AD 270. Here ends the life of Saint Pelagia.

3 Satan blames the bishop for stealing his "mistress" and being in opposition to him. His use of "old crooked fellow" is amusing because that was usually how the devil was described.

Saint Margaret Pelagia

Not to be confused with the life of Saint Margaret of Antioch, this legend makes no reference to another source besides Jacobus, and it follows the same tradition as Saint Pelagia. Jacobus does not give any indication about the origins of this legend or that of Saint Pelagia, which bears some resemblance to Margaret of Antioch as well. Jacobus says the legend of Saint Margaret of Antioch was written by "Theotimus, a learned man" but gives no other clue to his identity. This Margaret, who was swallowed by a dragon that burst asunder at the sign of the cross, is a much more powerful figure than Margaret Pelagia. While Margaret Pelagia is not nearly as outspoken or defiant as her sister saint, her life does prove an interesting twist in the story of the holy transvestites. Unlike Marina, she is not an innocent child raised as a boy, nor is she a repentant sinner like Theodora and Pelagia. She runs off to a monastery to avoid marriage, the consequences of which she is fully aware of, and while she is living as a man, she is chosen for a position of power as the head of a neighboring nunnery. This is the only instance where a woman, dressed as a man, is installed as the head of a convent and then accused of getting a young nun pregnant. The circumstances of her legend, while similar to those of the other transvestites falsely accused of paternity, present an interesting problem that was prevalent in the Middle Ages: What happens when you have a man in control of a house full of young virgins? The author of the legend makes it perfectly clear; these women were terrified of this man and feared that he would prey on their chastity next. Perhaps this legend, while a mirror image in many ways to the life of Pelagia, makes a subtle commentary about the way medieval nunneries were governed. Even though Margaret is later vindicated by her own admission of her true gender, the question remains: Was there a basis for suspicion among nuns that their male governors would take advantage of their position and endanger their chastity?[1] Or is it a comment on the

1 For more on nuns and their male governors, see *Visitations of Religious Houses in the Diocese of Lincoln*, ed. A. Hamilton Thompson, 3 vols. (London: Canterbury and York Society, 1915–27).

dangers of having nuns and monks who cohabited in joint houses and perhaps did not follow the rules of their order regarding chastity? Margaret's punishment is unjust; the author says that "he was thrown out without knowing why," and she is enclosed like a recluse, though her confinement is not voluntary like Pelagia's. There is also no mention of how she raised the child in great humility, like Marina. This is the most active case of injustice, which leads to her death and discovery. Whereas Eugenia rips her clothing off in public to reveal her true gender and therefore her innocence, Margaret writes it out in a letter addressed to the abbot. She is one of the few examples in the *Gilte Legende* of a woman who voices her defiance in written words as opposed to spoken debate. In light of these marked differences, Margaret Pelagia's legend provides another example of the trend of holy transvestitism and its impact on hagiographic literature. While these women are bound together by the manner of their devotion and by the rejection of their gender, their sanctity manifests itself in different ways: some are silent, some vocal, some innocent of their true nature; others are repentant sinners trying to efface their sin by masking their sex. The issue of transvestitism in the early Christian texts raises a number of questions regarding the perception of women and the idea of sexual identity; as the saints' gender changes, so does our perception of the role of women in medieval hagiography.

The Life of Saint Margaret Pelagia

Margaret, who is called Pelagia, was a noble and fair virgin full of riches. She was nobly and curiously kept so that she was taught to keep all sorts of good manners. She was so attentive in keeping honesty and chastity that she refused to be seen among men in any way. But at last a young noble man desired her, and by the accord of some of her kin everything was arranged for her marriage feast with great glory and great riches. When the wedding day arrived on which this young man and this maid were assembled with great nobility before the chamber where her kindred had prepared the wedding feast with such great joy and solemnity, this holy virgin, inspired by God, considered how the damage and loss of her virginity would be brought about with harmful rejoicing. She fell down to the earth in tears and began to think in her heart about the recompense of her virginity and the sorrows that followed weddings so that she accounted all the joys of this as nothing. That night she kept herself from her husband, and at midnight she commended herself to God, cut off her hair, dressed herself in men's clothing, and fled far into a monastery of monks and called herself Pelagian. There she was received by the abbot and taught diligently. She bore herself with holiness and religion.

When the ruler and keeper of a nearby nunnery died, by the counsel of the abbot Pelagian was made master of the abbey of nuns, though he would have greatly refused it. As he administered to them, not only their bodily necessities but also sacred, heavenly food continually and blamelessly, the fiend grew envious of his great virtue and thought how he might destroy his good name by some sinful action. As he thought, he formed his cursed purpose; a virgin who dwelled outside the gates committed adultery at the instigation of the fiend so that her womb rose and she could no longer hide it. All the virgins were so shamefast and so afraid of all the monks of that other abbey that they did not know what to do and believed truly that Pelagian, who was the provost and familiar with the virgins, had done this, and he was condemned by all without judgment. He was thrown out without knowing why and was shut up in a cave.

The cruelest of the monks was ordained to minister to him, and he served him with barley bread and water, and only in very small quantities. When the monks had enclosed him, they went their way, and left Pelagian all alone. He meekly and patiently endured and suffered all these wrongs and was not troubled by anything, but he always heartily loved and thanked God, and comforted himself in his chastity, following the examples of the saints.

At the end, when she knew that her death was near, she wrote letters to the abbot and the monks in this manner: "I, of noble kindred, was called Margaret in the world. But because I wished to eschew the temptations of the world, I called myself Pelagian. I am a woman. I have not lied to deceive because I have showed that I have the virtue of a man, and I have had virtue from the crime that was put upon me, and I, innocent of that, have done the penance. But I pray you, for as much as men did not know I was a woman, let the holy sisters bury my body so that the sight of my death may cleanse my life and the women will know I am a virgin whom they judged as an adulterer." When the abbot heard these things, the monks and the nuns ran to the pit where she was enclosed, and the women knew that she was a woman and a pure virgin untouched by man. They all did penance for the wrong they had done her and buried her holy body worshipfully among the virgins. Here ends the life of Margaret Pelagia.

Interpretive Essay

Silence and Speech in the Female Lives of the *Gilte Legende* and Their Influence on the Lives of Ordinary Medieval Women

The legends of female saints were only one form of literary expression during the Middle Ages, but aside from communicating the glorious and exaggerated deeds of the saints, they served as instructional texts for women from all walks of life. They were part of the "new behavioral model" presented to women by clerics "in the hope that authority handed down from the past would help it function in the present and continue to do so in the future."[1] These accounts constitute a small portion of the hagiography that began during the first Christian centuries and continued through the course of the medieval period, but their influence was widely felt. These texts were intended for a diverse female audience, and the subject matter suited the various roles assigned to women in society; powerful women who through their vocal protests or quiet submission challenged the patriarchal social and political structure. Teresa Coletti points out that,

> Recent studies of these hagiographical texts by Sheila Delany and Karen Winstead provide a detailed picture of the ways in which authors sought to model their subjects in accordance with the values and aspirations of their well-to-do patrons even as they engaged social, religious, and political issues that were relevant both to communities of lay readers and to the fortunes of church and nation.[2]

1 Carla Casagrande, "The Protected Woman" in *A History of Women in the West, vol. II: Silences of the Middle Ages*, ed. Christiane Klapisch-Zuber (Cambridge, Mass.: Belknap Press of Harvard University Press, 1992) p. 72.

2 Teresa Coletti, "Paupertas est donum Dei: Hagiography, Lay Religion, and the Economics of Salvation in the Digby *Mary Magdalene*," *Speculum* 76, no. 2 (2001) p. 343. Coletti is referring to Sheila Delany, *Impolitic Bodies: Poetry, Saints and Society in Fifteenth-Century England* (Oxford: Oxford University Press, 1998) and Karen Winstead, *Virgin Martyrs: Legends of Sainthood in Late Medieval England* (Ithaca: Cornell University Press, 1997).

Women appeared in a number of different texts, both pastoral and instructional, for the purpose of educating the female population, "They were present in great numbers; all of them. The education of women was particularly ambitious. Preachers were not satisfied to speak to just some of them – either because they were high up on the social scale or dedicated themselves to a holy and virtuous life. The challenge was to develop a model applicable to all women, at all times."[3] The lives of women saints occupy a special place in this body of instructional literature because they presented women in the Middle Ages with a selection of diverse examples: strong-minded, strong-willed women who face death and defilement with a defiance that belies their "fragile sex," or dictates the course of their lives through dramatic decisions. While women could rely on the male perception of "the fragility of her sex" to confine them to certain submissive roles, that same "fragility" could also provide protection or allow women to escape the consequences of their actions, giving them a greater amount of freedom based on the infirmity that was supposed to keep them obedient.[4] Women could use that status to their advantage, just as they could use the pious, decorous models set before them as examples of independence, regardless of male authors' intentions.

The legends of female saints, especially in vernacular collections like the *Gilte Legende*, provided strong, visible role models for medieval women through the diversity of their speech and the eloquence of their silence, elevating women above the traditional roles assigned to them and giving them a power of their own. "Many more saints' lives were written for and owned, heard or read, or, in the case of some anonymous works, possibly composed, by women. . . . Beyond these sources again there is much evidence from material culture testifying to women as patrons, devotees, and clients of saints."[5] Saint Christina, a virgin martyr, stands out as one of the most vocal advocates for her sex and her religion. Mary Magdalene redeemed the "original sin" of her gender, becoming one of the most venerated and outspoken examples of female sanctity in the medieval period. Saintly wives and mothers, like Elizabeth of Hungary and Paula, exercise their power, not through open confrontation but by

3 Casagrande, "The Protected Woman," p. 73.

4 C. E. Meek and M. K. Simms, *"The Fragility of Her Sex?": Medieval Irish Women in Their European Context* (Dublin: Four Courts Press, 1996) p. 8.

5 Jocelyn Wogan-Browne, *Saints' Lives and Women's Literary Culture: Virginity and its Authorizations* (Oxford: Oxford University Press, 2001) p. 3.

renouncing their traditional roles, while women like Theodora deny their gender and live as men, defying the conventions of female piety. The voice of the women in these texts had a profound impact on the lives of ordinary medieval women who read them, heard them, commissioned them, and preserved them in private collections like Osbern Bokenham's *Legendys of Hooly Wummen* and the *Gilte Legende*.

In medieval England the Middle English *Gilte Legende* was one of the most popular collections of hagiography. These legends were widely circulated and widely read by a secular society as well as those in religious communities. Unlike the rulebooks for women, such as the *Ancrene Wisse*, these legends were exciting and unusual, recording deeds that were miraculous and extraordinary. They chronicle legends of sacrifice and torture in the face of tyranny as well as religious devotion. The authors of these collections knew they would have a definite appeal to female audiences and so used them to instill an idea of perfect devotion, while providing stimulating subject matter. "Often, then, the legends worked not to propagate enduring values of Christianity but to invest partisan views on topical issues with the authority of tradition."[6] Scribes and translators adapted earlier texts to fit their own contexts and to serve their own agendas. The dialogue of these women saints is one of the most interesting parts of these legends and paints a dynamic portrait of their martyrdom, more so than silent submission. Their speech redeems them at the hands of their persecutors.

Another collection of female hagiography that played a prominent role in influencing the lives of medieval English women is the *Legendys of Hooly Wummen* written by Osbern Bokenham. It is clear that Bokenham's audience included a diverse selection of women, many of whom were in a position to own and distribute books. Bokenham reconstructed his work largely depending on his female audience; he changed the texts and used them as gentle instruction manuals,

> His admiring and chivalrous stance ensures that he is distanced from his subject, while his repetitive praise and constant reference to gender simultaneously protect and demean. At the same time, his apologies to his largely female audience permit him to offer a model of both feminine and holy behaviour for them to emulate. Bokenham

6 Winstead, *Virgin Martyrs*, p. 5.

> reveals an acute understanding of his medieval world, his texts exemplifying all the features of late medieval religious life, in particular those virtues such as patience and humility so prevalent amongst women. Apparently anxious to please an audience which shares this understanding, he makes important additions to his Latin sources.[7]

Bokenham obviously felt it necessary to appeal to women, even though he adopts a patronizing tone; he reworked his material significantly to satisfy his female patrons and provide viable models for them, at their request. It is possible that Bokenham used a Middle English source in addition to a Latin original; or perhaps he used a Middle English source in favor of a Latin exemplar, not because he had difficulty with the language but because his patron already had a version in her possession. The fragment bound with excerpts of the *Gilte Legende* that now makes up Trinity College, Dublin MS 319 (TCD MS 319) contains *Dorothy*, the translation of which is included in this edition, and *Catherine*, and it may have been owned by one of Bokenham's female patrons who gave it to him as an exemplar to use in his compilation. According to Richard Hamer and Vida Russell in their edition of the supplemental lives of the *Gilte Legende*, the legend of Saint Dorothy exists in three different forms in at least eight different manuscripts.[8] The distribution of these manuscripts shows how available these texts were to women who, by the fifteenth century, were literate and influential. The Trinity manuscript contains one of the few surviving versions of the life of Saint Dorothy and a version of *Catherine* that is not in the original *Legenda Aurea*, suggesting that the legends were adapted for a singular purpose or audience.

The copy of the *Gilte Legende* in TCD MS 319 with selections textually similar to Bokenham gives a clearer picture of how books were kept and used in the individual home – and perhaps who was responsible for them. An important part of the history of this manuscript is the identity of its owners.[9] Bokenham dedicates his version

7 Gail Ashton, *The Generation of Identity in Late Medieval Hagiography: Speaking the Saint* (London: Routledge, 2000) p. 35.

8 Richard Hamer and Vida Russell, *Supplementary Lives in Some Manuscripts of the "Gilte Legende"* Early English Text Society, original series 315 (Oxford: Oxford University Press, 2000) p. xvi.

9 For further examples of women as book owners, see Susan Groag Bell, "Medieval Women Book Owners: Arbiters of Lay Piety and Ambassadors of Culture" in *Women and Power in the Middle Ages*, ed. Mary Erler and Maryanne Kowaleski

of *Dorothy* to John Hunt and his wife Isabel, about whom nothing is known except that "Hunt" is common in Suffolk records of the fifteenth century.[10] Isabel may have owned the fragment, given it to Bokenham to adapt into verse, and then discarded the segment because it was incomplete or, more likely, had it bound with another incomplete fragment of saints' lives from the *Gilte Legende* simply because of the similar subject matter. The name Kathryn Walsh appears twice in the manuscript, both times neatly written in a late-fifteenth-century hand in the margin of folio 57r. Kathryn Walsh is a mystery in the medieval records, but she may have been the daughter of a merchant who was given the book as a means of learning to read or as an example of how to live a pious life. It is possible that she was a resident in the home of one of Bokenham's patrons: a foster daughter or ward. Lesley Smith points out that there are numerous depictions in manuscripts of women with books or reading, and that this indicates a widespread literacy among the upper classes of women. "Educated daughters of wealthier families appear to have been taught reading and a little Latin like sons."[11] The monograph of Kathryn Walsh also provides a clue to ownership. While the identity of this woman is unknown, it is clear that she owned the book, or at least had access to it and used it. There are other examples of marginalia and other names written during the long history of this manuscript, but its female owner provides a different kind of insight into the life of this book, before and after the two fragments were bound together. At least one woman owned this book and left her imprint upon it, but it is not a lavish manuscript so it was most likely not part of a prized collection kept by a noble woman; it must have resided in a more ordinary household. Women

(Athens: University of Georgia Press, 1988); Anne Dutton, "Passing the Book: Testamentary Transmission of Religious Literature to and by Women in England, 1350–1500" in *Women, the Book and the Godly*, ed. Lesley Smith and Jane H. M. Taylor (Cambridge: D. S. Brewer, 1995); Felicity Riddy, "Women Talking about the Things of God: a Late Medieval Sub-Culture" in *Women and Literature in Britain, 1150–1500*, ed. Carol M. Meale (Berkeley: University of California Press, 1993); Ralph Hanna, "Some Norfolk Women and Their Books" in *The Cultural Patronage of Medieval Women*, ed. June Hall McCash (Athens: University of Georgia Press, 1996).

10 Osbern Bokenham, *Legendys of Hooly Wummen*, ed. Mary Serjeantson, Early English Text Society, original series 206 (Oxford: Oxford University Press, 1938) pp. xx, xxi.

11 Lesley Smith, "Scriba Femina: Medieval Depictions of Women Writing" in *Women and the Book: Assessing the Visual Evidence*, ed. Smith (London: British Library, 1997) p. 23.

were much more involved in the compilation and transmission of texts than many people think, and TCD MS 319 provides a clear example of that tradition. "The presence and probable influence of women in the beginnings of vernacular literatures, particularly Provençal and French, have been much discussed, but the fact that women also influenced literature in Latin, religious and secular, throughout the Middle Ages, probably more than we can trace, has had less attention."[12] However this manuscript survived, it is clear that the two halves of this book, containing the legends of five women saints out of a total nineteen, passed through many hands, male and female, and was heavily used. This specific manuscript gives a clearer picture of the influence this book and its owners may have had on the composition of one of the most widely circulated pieces of English vernacular religious poetry of the Middle Ages.

Sheila Delany makes a case for the separate and independent circulation of Bokenham's legends, including Saints Dorothy and Catherine. She says Bokenham used Jacobus's *Legenda Aurea* as his primary source, though *Dorothy* does not appear in the *Legenda Aurea*, and adapted his material to fit his predominantly female audience,

> While working within a narrowly defined genre with well-known stories, Bokenham is no mere copyist. He does not simply transcribe his main source, the thirteenth-century *Legenda Aurea*, nor only imitate English collections such as the *South English Legendary.* Everywhere Bokenham reworks the material, reshaping it according to his own vision.[13]

Bokenham's use of the traditional hagiography in special collections designed and rewritten for women illustrates the importance of these legends in the everyday lives of medieval women. Although the texts were written and transmitted by clerics, they were considered texts for women, both secular and religious. Therefore the strident speeches given to the virgin martyrs, Mary Magdalene, and the silent mutiny of Elizabeth could not be accidental. Bokenham knew his audience and he chose material that would appeal to them and serve as a model for their lives.

12 Joan Ferrante, *To the Glory of Her Sex: Women's Roles in the Composition of Medieval Texts* (Indianapolis: Indiana University Press, 1997) p. 39.

13 Sheila Delany, introduction to *Legends of Holy Women: A Translation of Osbern Bokenham's "Legendys of Hooly Wummen"* (Notre Dame, Ind.: University of Notre Dame Press, 1992) p. xxxi. Also see: Sheila Delany, *Impolitic Bodies*. Cf. note 2.

Despite the evidence that women were the intended audience for a large portion of this material, there has been a great deal of debate about how much these texts reflect the actual voice of women, because they were transmitted primarily through a male pen. Monique Alexandre contends, "women's voices are rarely heard . . . the only vision of women to which we have access is the idealized normative one put forward by clerics and monks."[14] Georges Duby and Michelle Perrot assert that women were destined for "silent" roles; motherhood and homemaking, "tasks relegated to the obscurity of a domesticity that did not count and was not considered worth recounting."[15] However, Duby and Perrot also note that "religious writing was another form of expression open to women. We can hear the voices of renowned saints, mystics and abbesses."[16] The legends of women saints are part of that religious expression, even though they were written largely by men. Women play a very powerful part in the hagiographical tradition, illustrated by the four distinct categories of female saints in this volume; the voice of women resonates in these texts, influencing a medieval audience that was increasingly female. Martha Driver explains, "By the end of the fourteenth century, women were increasingly literate, educated to assist in family business, keep the books, manage the household, help with correspondence and teach their children."[17] There were a number of literate women in both the upper and middle classes who probably owned books of their own. In *The Book of the City of Ladies*, published in 1405, Christine de Pizan talks about sitting in her study surrounded by her books.[18] According to Natalie Zemon Davis, Christine had her manuscripts copied and illuminated in all-female workshops,[19] and she remains a visible example of book production

14 Monique Alexandre, "Early Christian Women" in Pauline Schmitt Pantel, ed., *A History of Women in the West, vol. I: From Ancient Goddesses to Christian Saints* (Cambridge, Mass.: Harvard University Press, 1992) p. 412.

15 Georges Duby and Michelle Perrot, "Writing the History of Women" in Pauline Schmitt Pantel, ed., *A History of Women in the West, vol. I: From Ancient Goddesses to Christian Saints*, p. ix.

16 Duby and Perrot, "Writing the History of Women," p. xiv.

17 Martha Driver, "Mirrors of a Collective Past: Reconsidering Images of Medieval Women" in Smith ed., *Women and the Book*, p. 75.

18 Christine de Pizan, *The Book of the City of Ladies*, translated by Earl Jeffrey Richards (New York: Persea Books, 1998) p. 3.

19 Natalie Zemon Davis, forward to *The Book of the City of Ladies* by Christine de Pizan, p. xvi. Lesley Smith also addresses the question of female workshops in her article "Scriba Femina," in *Women and the Book: Assessing the Visual Evidence*, pp. 23, 27. Smith notes that some nuns were trained as scribes and that Christine de

and ownership among women, especially those of the higher classes. Eleanor of Aquitaine was also a notable collector of books and a patron of women like Marie de France, who wrote for the court of Henry II. By the fifteenth century, more women had access to books and were acquiring libraries and collections of their own. The continued existence of hagiographical collections in Latin and the European vernaculars, including the Middle English *Gilte Legende*, is a testament to their popularity and range of dissemination, showing how influential the legends of women saints were in medieval society and to their female audience.

Most of these saints' lives were written by identifiable male authors; according to the *Bibliotheca Hagiographica Latina,* for the years 500 to 1100, thirty-nine percent of the female lives have identifiable authors, all of whom were male except two.[20] Male ecclesiastical authors, though they may have been concerned with the lasting obedience and silence of women, gave their female saints a vocal presence in their legends. While it may be the voice of Christian doctrine providing examples of sanctity for general edification, the women saints are allowed to speak for themselves. The dialogue in the legends, especially those of the virgin martyrs, gives the impression that it is not merely the voice of a male biographer that is being heard. The women are largely historical inventions constructed as representations of sanctity, but the fact that they speak clearly and loudly for themselves, instead of having their message conveyed by a male narrator, shows the female voice is an integral part of hagiography. Joan Ferrante notes that it is precisely because men respected certain women that these accounts survive, "Some of the men around them recognized and encouraged them, and it is because they recognized and encouraged them that we have, in many cases, any record of that achievement at all."[21] These legends may not be accurate accounts of female speech because their historical content is questionable, but many of the stories indicate that women were respected for their speech and religious expression. According to Catherine Mooney, "Male manipulation of female texts and saintly portrayals

Pizan used a notable female illuminator named Anastasia to illustrate her work. She also suggests that Christine de Pizan may have been trained in one of these workshops.

20 Jane Tibbetts Schulenberg, "Saints' Lives as a Source for the History of Women, 500–1100" in *Medieval Women and the Sources of Medieval History*, ed. Joel T. Rosenthal (Athens: University of Georgia Press, 1990) p. 291.

21 Ferrante, *To the Glory of Her Sex*, p. 7.

endured long after the saints and their original interpreters had completed their texts and died."[22] In most cases, men controlled the content of these saints' legends and, therefore, controlled the character of the saint themselves: "Women's words almost invariably reach us only after having passed through the filter of their male confessors, patrons, and scribes."[23] However, if men were solely bent on subjugating women through the transmission and adaptation of these texts, then the vocal accounts of female defiance would have been muted or omitted, which they are not, especially in the legends of virgin martyrs.

But there are other, less vocal, representations of female rebellion. The life of Elizabeth of Hungary is a powerful example of a woman who was totally under male domination. Her confessor dictates her actions, devotion, and limited speech. He has utter control over her faith and later her sanctity – control that Elizabeth accepts willingly. The striking difference between Elizabeth and her early Christian predecessors is that she has no means by which to prove her sanctity other than obedience; martyrdom is not an option since Christianity was firmly established by the thirteenth century. Her legend highlights the shift from the vocal, defiant saints of the early Christian period to the quiet, demure, saintly women of the medieval period. Elizabeth has virtually no voice of her own, even though the women she was taught to emulate were extremely outspoken, but that does not mean Elizabeth was not a strong female role model for women of the Middle Ages. Her strength and power lie in her decision to give up the secular life. Elizabeth's adherence to the spiritual control of Conrad defies the conventions of her social position and her family obligations. This is exemplified by Paula's rejection of her children in favor of a contemplative life and the rejection of the female gender by the repentant transvestites, like Theodora, as a means of erasing their sin. These saints were venerated for denying their natural gender or their maternal instincts, but they still serve as examples of powerful women because they make the choice, whatever the consequences. Paula chooses to abandon her children to travel as a pilgrim and, however repugnant that decision may seem to a modern audience, in the medieval context she made what would have been

22 Catherine Mooney, *Gendered Voices: Medieval Saints and Their Interpreters* (Philadelphia: University of Pennsylvania Press, 1999) p. 9.

23 Mooney, *Gendered Voices*, p. 7.

considered one of the most difficult and heart-rending choices, though as a saint she is venerated "despite rather than because of her children."[24] While it is ironic that her sanctity is based on the desertion of her "natural" identity, she makes her decision of her own free will and dictates the path her life will take, just like Elizabeth who places her life and soul under Conrad's control. All of the female transvestites except Marina, who most likely had no concept of gender and lived an asexual life, choose to discard their female identity as their punishment for sexual transgressions. Each decides to cast away her former self and, in doing so, casts away her former life and sin. Though they are at the mercy of cruel clerics, these transvestites place themselves there willingly. It would have been just as acceptable for these women to place themselves under the authority of a convent; instead, they enter monasteries and expunge what they see as the very cause of their transgression.

The speeches and outbursts of the women of the *Gilte Legende* should not be dismissed because they survive through the writings of men. Nor should the silence of saints like Elizabeth and Paula relegate them to the status of oppressed women. The idea of female fragility and incompetence "reflects, of course, the views of men in the Middle Ages on the role and position of women, views not always borne out by their encounters with the opposite sex in real life."[25] Elizabeth is one of the most fragile saints in her utter submission to her confessor, but her biographer may have changed her story to fit an ideal, one that bore little resemblance to reality. Mooney points out that most clerical writers were much more than scribes or translators, even when they protested that they were only that.[26] If men invented these powerful women, they must have done so for a purpose, lifting women from their socially proscribed positions to a venerated status visible to most medieval communities. This strong, intelligent, articulate, and authoritative voice is so striking in the case of female saints precisely because they were not expected to have one, just as Elizabeth's rebellion against secular society for religious asceticism is daring and unconventional.

The virgin Saint Christina, whose father tortures her for her

24 Anneke Mulder-Bakker, *Sanctity and Motherhood: Essays on Holy Mothers in the Middle Ages* (New York: Garland, 1995) p. 4.

25 Meek and Simms, *"The Fragility of Her Sex?"*, p. 8.

26 Meek and Simms, *"The Fragility of Her Sex?"*, p. 8.

Christian beliefs, defends her body and her religion and is one of the most forceful and vocal saints included in the *Gilte Legende*. She challenges not only the authority of the Roman prelates but also the paternal authority wielded by her father: "Oh thou without worship or shame, and abominable to God, see you not how they have fallen? Pray to your gods that give them virtue and strength" (36). The *Life of Saint Christina*, though very brief, has a great deal of forceful, aggressive dialogue between Saint Christina and her various tormentors. For a female saint, whose role as a woman is traditionally one of silence, her speech elevates her above the societal constraints of her gender.

Christina's speech is authoritative enough to overthrow pagan gods, drive out serpents – the symbols of Satan and the fall – and raise the dead: "She raised the dead man from death to life" (37). In an unusual twist, Christina does not supplicate Christ to do her will by praying. Her prayers are never mentioned; she demonstrates her own ability and authority to carry out God's will through her speech. Julian commands that her tongue be cut out because it appears to be the root of her power but significantly that does not stop her from speaking, preaching, and blinding him: "After that, he made them cut out her tongue, but she never lost her power of speech, instead she took the piece of her tongue that they cut off, threw it in the judge's face, and struck out both his eyes with it" (38).

The power of her speech is emphasized by this act and by her role as a preacher. She preaches to her father the notion of the Trinity after he who is "unkunnynge," or without the ability to understand, questions the existence of one God. She preaches to her father many times; condemning his worship and him as a product of the devil, and delighting in the fact that he disowns her for not performing a sacrifice: "Now you have done me a great grace since I shall no longer be called the devil's daughter, for he that is born of the devil is the devil, and you are the father of that same evil" (36).

She curses him and taunts him to eat the flesh that he has begotten, after he has it torn from her body. After giving the order to have her beheaded, he is found dead. She is strong and powerful in her speech, her actions, and therefore her holiness. Christina does not succumb meekly to the blow of the executioner but must be grievously tortured and shot with arrows before she finally receives her crown of martyrdom – and even when she is being boiled, her voice triumphs as she sings with angels for five days. In her unwavering devotion and relentless defiance, Christina becomes a shield for Christianity, a steadfast line of defense in the face of pagan persecution, like all virgin martyrs of her time whose lives were recorded as hagiography.[27]

Giving this young woman such a powerful presence and vehement authority raises the question of how women were supposed to behave in medieval society, and whether women like Christina were examples of an unobtainable ideal.

> Although opportunities for women's eloquence are less formally offered and less well-resourced . . . the rhetorical positions available in saints' lives are unlikely to have been any less encouraging to verbal play and fantasy. It is difficult to believe that the represented denunciation, defiance, prayer, and asseveration in saints' lives offered no models of pleasure and plenitude in speech to their female audiences. For those without access to Latin classes on Ovidian and other classical heroines, vernacular saints' lives constitute a repertoire of authorized speeches by women.[28]

Women were imbued with such force to enhance their sainthood; no ordinary woman could be a saint, they had to be extraordinary, even more so than their male counterparts, and in being so outstanding, they shone as examples for a female audience that could only aspire to their sanctity and independence. Women who were more assertive in their religious roles were generally viewed as mystical and mysterious.[29] This awe made the women in question objects of veneration precisely because they were different. Praise from a hagiographer could be a double-edged sword, however: "In their praise of women, many ecclesiastical writers of the Middle Ages expressed similar sentiments regarding some women's special ability to deny or transcend the 'natural frailty' of their own sex; this type of behavior set them apart from ordinary women and singled them out as candidates for sainthood."[30] The legends may have been intended only as educational tools for women – a demonstration of piety for them to aspire to, but they also demonstrated independence in speech and thought, necessary in the changing world when societal roles of women were becoming more prominent and powerful. "Women's public speech is represented in a number of ways during the period, perhaps nowhere

27 Kathleen Coyne Kelly, *Performing Virginity and Testing Chastity in the Middle Ages* (London: Routledge, 2000) p. 13.

28 Wogan-Browne, *Saints' Lives and Women's Literary Culture*, p. 225.

29 Meek and Simms, *"The Fragility of Her Sex?"*, p. 10.

30 Jane Tibbetts Schulenburg, *Forgetful of Their Sex: Female Sanctity and Society ca. 500–1100* (Chicago: University of Chicago Press, 1998) p. 1.

more luxuriantly than in saints' lives."[31] Letters and secular records show that women were a visible part of society and that they looked to these aggressive saints as their models. "What is particularly striking in the letters and in texts commissioned by women is how much women, even those playing male roles in secular government or rising above sex in their religious lives, are aware of themselves as women and identify with powerful or effective, not oppressed, women in history."[32] There were many women to choose from in the collections of hagiography. Christina is only one of these examples, and her legend illustrates how speech is used as an implement of power in the lives of the female saints in the *Gilte Legende*. Saint Margaret of Antioch defends herself against the fiend and stamps on his neck, drawing on imagery from Genesis about crushing the serpent, while he wails, "Ah blessed virgin Margaret, I am overcome. If a young man had beaten me I would not have given it a second thought. But I have been vanquished by a young, tender maid, and for that I am sorrowful because her father and mother have been my good friends" (54). She constrains him forcibly, interrogating him until he tells her the truth of his temptations, and she is able to dispel him with her command: "Flee, you wretched demon!" (55). She proves her holiness through her speech, which is powerful enough to command and control demons and drive them away. Margaret and the other virgin saints exercise their divine authority, manifested in their speech, validating them as individual examples, and there is "no question that hagiography, like sermons, influenced the spiritual and devotional lives of the people of the Middle Ages. There are countless examples of medieval people whose religious lives were significantly altered after having encountered a particular saint's life."[33] Each woman could find her own saint and take what message she wanted from her legend, emulating any part of that saint's life that applied to her own.

One of the most influential saints in the medieval period was Mary Magdalene, who is described as a preacher, converting large numbers of people by the authority of her speech, including the Prince of Marseilles. He challenges her to defend her preaching, and she replies, "Surely, I am ready to defend it as she who is confirmed

31 Wogan-Browne, *Saints' Lives and Women's Literary Culture*, p. 223.

32 Ferrante, *To the Glory of Her Sex*, p. 7.

33 Katherine Ludwig Jansen, *The Making of the Magdalen: Preaching and Popular Devotion in the Later Middle Ages* (Princeton: Princeton University Press, 2000) p. 9.

every day by miracles and by the predication of our master Saint Peter who sits in the see of Rome" (91). According to her legend, it is only fitting for Mary Magdalene to spread the Word of God because she washed his feet with her kisses and wiped them with her hair; it "was no wonder the mouth that had so debonairly and so goodly kissed the feet of our Lord was more inspired by the word of God than any other" (90). Her speech is an incremental part of her sanctity, even though the woman venerated in the Middle Ages bore little resemblance to the historical figure.

The Mary Magdalene who appears in the *Gilte Legende* and the mystery plays is actually a composite of three women, according to Jacques Dalarun. This combination – of Mary of Magdala, who, healed of the seven devils by Christ, became his disciple and followed him to Calvary to be the first witness of the Resurrection; of Mary of Bethany, the sister of Martha and Lazarus; and of the anonymous woman sinner (the "Sinner of the City") who, at the home of Simon Pharisee, "moistens Christ's feet with her tears, wipes them with her hair, covers them with her kisses and anoints them with perfume"[34] – became the venerated female figure in the Middle Ages. Gregory the Great is responsible for first combining the images of the three women into the popular figure of Christ's lover, companion, and preacher: Mary Magdalene. It is this tripartite figure that appears in the mystery cycles and the corpus of saints' lives, including the *Gilte Legende*. She is the one to whom the news of the Resurrection is first given for dissemination, and who is elected as the bishop of Marseilles after converting the prince and princess, saving their lives and souls through a number of miracles. The medieval manifestation of Mary Magdalene is much stronger and more prominent than the biblical model; Mary Magdalene changed as the roles and perceptions of women changed, diversifying and becoming a virtuous but powerful icon wielding the vocal authority of God.

The Bible does not mention the actual words spoken by Mary Magdalene, except in the Gospel of Saint John; each tells a different version of the story, but the other three consistently omit her dialogue.[35] According to the Gospel of Saint Mark, Jesus appears to Mary Magdalene with angels, and later Jesus revalidates her right to

34 Jacques Dalarun, "The Clerical Gaze" in Klapisch-Zuber, ed., *A History of Women in the West, vol. II: Silences of the Middle Ages*, p. 32.

35 Matt. 27: 61, 28: 1–10; Mark 15: 47, 16: 1–15; Luke 24: 10–11; John 19: 25–7, 20:

preach his message while chastising the apostles for doubting her word, but does give the text of what she says.[36] The Gospel of Saint Luke does not name Mary Magdalene at first and has many women spreading the news of the Resurrection,[37] while Saint Matthew speaks of two Marys delivering the news.[38] Mary Magdalene is identified in the Gospel of Saint John, and it is clear that Christ instructs her to speak. Jesus speaks to the disciples directly after her, blending the two together as though he is speaking through her,

> Jesus saith to her: "Mary." She turning, saith to him: "Rabboni" (which is to say, Master). Jesus saith to her: "Do not touch me, for I am not yet ascended to my Father. But go to my brethren, and say to them: I ascend to my Father and to your Father, to my God and to your God." Mary Magdalen cometh, and telleth the disciples: "I have seen the Lord, and these things he said to me."[39]

In the Gnostic *Gospel According to Mary*, contemporary with the four Gospels of the New Testament, Christ appears to Mary in a vision, which she relates to the disciples using her own voice: "Then arose Mary, saluted them all, and spake to her brethren, 'Weep not, be not sorrowful neither be ye undecided, for his grace will be with you all and will protect you. Let us rather praise his greatness, for he hath made us ready, and made us to be men.'"[40] She speaks of the revelations she received from Christ, who "loved her above all other women."[41] However, Andrew and Peter question the validity of her vision and the other disciples rebuke them, highlighting Peter's hostility toward women and Mary Magdalene in particular:

> Then Mary wept and said to Peter: "My brother Peter, what dost thou then believe? Dost thou believe that I imagined this myself in my heart, or that I would lie about the Saviour?" Levi answered (and) said to Peter: "Peter, thou hast ever

1–19 (Holy Bible, Douay-Rheims version, revised by Bishop Richard Challoner, 1749–52).

36 Mark 16: 14.

37 Luke 24: 10.

38 Matt. 28: 1–10.

39 John 20: 16–18.

40 "The Gospel According to Mary" in *New Testament Apocrypha*, ed. Edgar Hennecke and Wilhelm Schneemelcher (London: Lutterworth Press, 1963) vol. 1, p. 342. It should be noted that Mary refers to herself as one of "men," a switch in gender that occurs in a few of the female saints' lives, particularly those that involve transvestitism.

41 "The Gospel According to Mary," vol. 1, p. 342.

> been of a hasty temper. Now I see how thou dost exercise thyself against the woman like the adversaries. But if the Saviour hath made her worthy, who then art thou, that thou reject her? Certainly the Saviour knows her surely enough. Therefore did he love her more than us."[42]

The lack of dialogue in the canonical text shows there is no biblical precedent for Mary Magdalene as a preacher or saintly figure; it is a medieval invention in its truest form that illustrates "the growth of legendary material all of which served to elaborate various aspects of Mary Magdalen's life which the Gospels had passed over in silence."[43] Mary Magdalene became a medieval icon because of this invention, especially for prostitutes, the only women who had any freedom outside the home and were recognized as independent of the family. They were assigned a separate place, but it was recommended that they "follow the comforting example of Mary Magdalene, abandon their shameful activity and dedicate themselves to a new penitent life."[44]

Despite the reinforcement of Mary Magdalene and other female saints as vocal defendants of the faith in the *Gilte Legende* there was serious opposition to women preaching, or even speaking in public: "One of the reasons usually given for the male monopoly on preaching was that a woman preacher, however virtuous, would incite immoral thoughts in her auditors. Speaking in public, she would compound her threat to men's souls."[45] The Bible specifically speaks against women preaching, as in the First Epistle of Saint Paul to the Corinthians: "Let women keep silence in the churches: for it is not permitted them to speak, but to be subject, as also the law saith. But if they would learn anything, let them ask their husbands at home. For it is a shame for a woman to speak in the church."[46] In the Middle Ages, before and during the time in which the *Gilte Legende* was being compiled and disseminated, biblical passages like this validated the view that women were inferior. However, the presence of literature describing women as vocal proponents of the faith cannot be ignored, "Recently scholars of early Christianity, particularly feminist scholars, have taken up the case of Mary Magdalen in an

42 "The Gospel According to Mary," vol. 1, pp. 343–4.

43 Jansen, *The Making of the Magdalen*, p. 20.

44 Casagrande, "The Protected Woman," p. 77.

45 Alcuin Blamires, *Woman Defamed and Woman Defended: An Anthology of Medieval Texts* (Oxford: Clarendon Press, 1992) p. 4.

46 Corinthians 14: 34–5.

effort to demonstrate the presence of authoritative female leaders in the early Christian Church."[47] This presence is in direct conflict with the goals of antifeminist clerics, such as Saint Augustine and Saint Jerome, who sought to keep Mary Magdalene out of popular devotion, except as a sinner who repents the error of her ways, and were determined to keep women out of the public arena, limiting their ability to speak.

Women play a prominent role in the *Gilte Legende*, but the example of the repentant sinner was reinforced by many patristic writers in the Middle Ages who wished to keep women in what they deemed their proper place: submissive and adhering to the virtues of humility, gentleness, and obedience. The clerics strove to achieve this by admonishing women who behaved otherwise in their sermons and through "prescriptive treatises." Carla Casagrande points out that Mary Magdalene was not always revered as a saint or as a model for medieval women to follow: "The adventurous alternative of independence – experienced, for example, by Mary Magdalene who, according to Jacobus of Voragine, was sinful and exerted a bad influence over other women because she was free and her own mistress (*sui domina et libera*) – was eyed with disapproval and suspicion."[48] However, Jacobus included the legend of an extremely powerful and vocal Mary Magdalene in the *Legenda Aurea* that became the standard account of her life circulated in the Middle Ages. Christine de Pizan attacked preachers who claimed that Christ chose to appear to Mary Magdalene after his resurrection because he knew that, being a woman, she would soon spread his word far and wide.[49] The antifeminist clerics supported the idea that women were not really preachers nor were they meant to be, not even the revered Mary Magdalene, but were simply gossips who delighted in spreading news without considering or understanding the value or implications of what they were saying. Dalarun points out that Geoffrey of Monmouth was writing for his monks, not for women, when he spoke of Mary Magdalene, and that she was to be venerated as a figure, not as a woman.[50] Patristic writers thought of her as the soul to man's spirit and held her up as a model for female sinners of the flesh, namely prostitutes, and not as a preacher spreading the Word of God. The image of Mary Magdalene in the Middle Ages is one

47 Jansen, *The Making of the Magdalen*, p. 12.
48 Casagrande, "The Protected Woman," pp. 90–1.
49 Casagrande, "The Protected Woman," p. 98.
50 Dalarun, "The Clerical Gaze," p. 124.

still tied to the form of her female flesh, an image from which she rarely escapes. But she became a powerful political figure in the Middle Ages as her character fluctuated from the ultimate sinner to the consummate saint, and her voice gained authority with the retelling of her tale. "The many Catherines and Magdalens of this period function as a locus for the politics of vernacular and lay, not only women's, speech. But in thematizing issues of church and clerical power these figures still represent copious and efficacious speech by women."[51] The account of her life in the version of the *Gilte Legende* found in TCD MS 319 makes it clear that not only was she a preacher but she was ordained the Bishop of Marseilles.[52] Katherine Ludwig Jansen notes that this combination is not unusual, "This heady mix of politics and sanctity was by no means uncommon in the Middle Ages . . . the historical record yielded a legendary saint whom the Middle Ages and subsequent generations venerated as Mary Magdalen, but doubtless a figure all but unrecognizable to her companions of the early Christian Church."[53] So regardless of Geoffrey of Monmouth's intention when writing for his monks in the twelfth century, the image of Mary Magdalene and what she represented changed drastically throughout the Middle Ages, providing a blueprint for women who read her legend and followed her example.

Mary Magdalene, more so than any other woman, illustrates how speech was an implement of power in medieval female hagiography precisely because she is an example of how widely the views of women as role models and religious icons differed in the Middle Ages and were often contradictory in a single text. Casagrande explains the importance of these texts in shaping the lives of medieval women,

> Among the many texts which for three centuries spoke to women about women, those composed between the end of the twelfth and the beginning of the fifteenth century were the most influential. In those years a serious attempt was made to set up a flexible ethical model suitable for women in

51 Wogan-Browne, *Saints' Lives and Women's Literary Culture*, p. 224.

52 Mary Magdalene is identified as the bishop of Marseilles in TCD MS 319. Osbern Bokenham and Jacobus de Voragine's *Legenda Aurea* have Lazarus ordained as the bishop of Marseilles, as do a number of other vernacular versions of her legend.

53 Jansen, *The Making of the Magdalen*, p. 19.

> an increasingly involved and differentiated society; a lasting pedagogical and pastoral foundation was laid.[54]

The texts of the *Gilte Legende* tell stories in which women speak for themselves of their passion, their love for God, and their place as his spouse and about how their words are instrumental in the conversion of thousands to the Christian faith. Women were essential in the early days of Christendom and were able to transcend the common strictures placed upon their sex in the name of the Christian cause,

> Through their aristocratic birth and exercise of autonomy and power, they formed an elite group who were singled out for their religious dedication and zeal. While the lives of these holy heroines do not seem to have been fully coterminus [sic] with the experiences of religious women in general, it appears that especially during the early stages of conversion to Christianity, when the nobility played a central role, there were a great many aristocratic women with more power and visibility in the church and society than usual. They were then rewarded for their leadership roles in the church by being elevated to sainthood. These female saints and their *vitae* therefore provided society with some idea of the ideals and the kind of life being practiced by this very special spiritual elite.[55]

The women of the *Gilte Legende* are predominantly early Christian saints and their legends take place in a time when women were instrumental in promoting the fledgling religion. Their speech was necessary, and it stands to reason that these are the women whom the Church Fathers would elevate as role models for the women of the Middle Ages. But in doing that, medieval women were presented with vocal, defiant role models that allowed them to reconsider their own position in society. By the medieval period, however, female speech was viewed with a certain amount of suspicion, even from the mouths of saints. "In the age of conversion, the word had unequivocally been the Word of God; by the twelfth and thirteenth centuries, words were recognized to be double-edged. Words could nourish faith; they could also destroy it: the cup of knowledge might turn out to be a poisoned chalice."[56]

54 Casagrande, "The Protected Woman," p. 71.

55 Tibbetts Schulenberg, "Saints' Lives as a Source for the History of Women," p. 307.

56 Henrietta Leyser, *Medieval Women: A Social History of Women in England, 450–1500* (London: Phoenix Grant, 1995) p. 197.

That poisoned chalice may not have been intended for female consumption, as the treatises against women reading and interpreting the Scriptures suggest, but women were a vital part of many religious communities and an attentive audience. Many male religious houses operated with a joint house for women close by and dependent – if not on the same premises – so the legends would have reached both religious audiences and provided models for pious women. These legends speak clearly of men and women spreading the faith together. "In the age of the conversion, holy men and women were, at least initially, committed to an enterprise of equal opportunity based on teaching and learning the new faith together."[57] As words developed a double edge, so did their use. Women spoke vehemently in their own words and defense, but the words were still largely dictated by men, especially in the case of such vocal role models as Mary Magdalene. These words filtered through the popular vernaculars of the time, including the Middle English *Gilte Legende*, changing their meaning, purpose, and educational effect. "[The Virgin] Mary of the Gospels is given only few words; those anxious to reinforce the Pauline message that women were to be silent in church found this a reassuring precedent. But for many late medieval men and women, the Virgin they knew stepped out of vernacular drama, not Latin Gospels."[58] The medieval depiction of the Virgin Mary and Mary Magdalene deviated from the traditional Pauline idea of silent, passive women, giving secular women authorized female examples of strength and defiance.

The female saints of the *Gilte Legende*, whose stories were compiled and translated from Latin into both French and English, also defied convention. The women in these legends are neither silent nor submissive to their antagonists, until Elizabeth of Hungary, whose life more closely follows the Pauline tradition. The secular accounts written by women like Christine de Pizan portray Elizabeth of Hungary as less of a model than saints like Christina or Dorothy who were more visible examples of sanctity and sacrifice, though Elizabeth's model was easier to follow and more practical. The legends of virgin martyrs were strikingly popular throughout the medieval period, however, because "the inconsistencies and ambiguities . . . allowed the virgin martyr legend, more than any other hagiographical genre, to mean different things to different people."[59]

57 Leyser, *Medieval Women*, p. 201.
58 Leyser, *Medieval Women*, p. 223.
59 Winstead, *Virgin Martyrs*, p. 5.

While the majority of the female audience for whom the legends were intended could not ascribe to the ideal of virgin martyrdom, they could take strength from the descriptions of their theological debates and their refusal to submit to their male persecutors. These legends had a significant impact on the everyday lives of women because they illustrate the importance of sanctity in the lives of women, and provide positive, assertive examples not tainted by the didactic intentions of some patristic writers. The legends are rarely definitive about anything; "rather, contradictory messages coexist, ready to be exploited to different ends."[60] Medieval women could interpret the legends according to their own position and find a voice in them. Danielle Rénier-Bohler points out that women spoke in private as well as public, exercising their "linguistic powers in a variety of ways, rich, subtle, and vehement; they spoke and they wrote."[61] The *Gilte Legende* acknowledges the real importance of women in medieval society by illuminating the role of women in the foundation of the early Christian church. Tibbetts Schulenburg says the Church used the saints' legends to promote passive virtues for women,[62] but the legends of saints such as Margaret of Antioch and Dorothy portray the majority of these women as neither passive nor submissive. However, they are virgin martyrs and their defiance is an integral part of their sanctity. For many women, the only option open to them was joining a religious community and renouncing their earthly life in favor of a strict, spiritual one – and not violent martyrdom.

Marina Warner points out, "Through the ascetic renunciation of the flesh, a woman could relieve a part of her nature's particular viciousness as the Virgin Mary had done through her complete purity. The life of self-denial was seen as a form of martyrdom, and the virgin was encouraged to suffer physically. . . . Through virginity and self-inflicted hardship, the faults of female nature could be corrected."[63] During the Middle Ages this form of asceticism was largely impractical and women were forced to rely on marriage or widowhood to attain some vestige of power. While virginity was

60 Winstead, *Virgin Martyrs*, p. 5.

61 Danielle Régnier-Bohler, "Literary and Mystical Voices" in Klapisch-Zuber, ed., *A History of Women in the West, vol. II: Silences of the Middle Ages*, p. 429.

62 Tibbetts Schulenburg, *Forgetful of Their Sex*, p. 7.

63 Marina Warner, *Alone of All Her Sex: The Myth and Cult of the Virgin Mary* (New York: Vintage Books, 1976) p. 69.

encouraged for daughters of all social strata, and practiced by those sent to convents and nunneries, there were other examples provided for those for whom voluntary virginity and martyrdom were impossible. Even though the virgin martyrs whose legends were disseminated were chaste and vocal, their example did not necessarily serve to exclude medieval women from the social and political arena.

Virgin saints, while the most numerous, are not the only women venerated in the corpus of hagiography. Wives, mothers, repentant sinners, and women who spent their lives disguised as men were also set up as legendary examples, which most likely influenced the ordinary lives of medieval women who did not take the veil. Christine de Pizan defends the role of women in spreading Christianity, citing non-virgin women, such as Clotilda, daughter of the king of Burgundy and wife of Clovis, king of France, who used their position as wife and queen to sway the opinions of those around them.[64] While the position of married women in hagiography is much lower than that of their virgin counterparts, a number of female saints were in fact married, "and it was within the context of marriage and the family that women, especially during the early Middle Ages, were able to play a crucial role within the Church and society – namely, that of 'domestic proselytizers.' "[65] In this way, saints such as Paula, even though she abandons her family after her husband's death in order to pursue an ascetic life, were models for married women in their fidelity. These women served a great purpose in the earliest days of Christianity, and that role carried over into the Middle Ages as women were seen as a means of persuading the people around them to carry on the religious tradition. Many of these women owned the collections of saints' legends and read them for inspiration and education, illustrated by the number of books dedicated to female patrons and the amount of literature written by women reflecting the lives of female saints.

The examples of strong defiant women in both the *Legendys of Hooly Wummen* and the *Gilte Legende* serve a much greater purpose, considering the control women actually exercised over their own education. Ferrante points out in her work on the epistolary tradition of women that women often wrote to religious men in the process of producing various works, and their questions and comments became instrumental in the composition of that work,

64 Christine de Pizan, *The Book of the City of Ladies*, II.35.1, p. 151.
65 Tibbetts Schulenburg, *Forgetful of Their Sex*, p. 177.

> The woman might set the man a program of activity, forcing him to work out his ideas or do more research, or she might frame the structure of his work by the questions she asked; and he responded because the subject interested him and he trusted her to be a sympathetic audience to ideas as he developed them or to be a purveyor of his ideas to a wider public. This led me to a much broader view of women's role in literature written by men, of collaboration as well as patronage.[66]

Women were often at the center of public life, their involvement determined more by their class than by their gender. They were actively involved in the management of households, the production of certain goods, religious contemplation and writing, and, in some cases, the governing of a country. While a misogynistic undercurrent existed in many aspects of medieval life, individual women were often elevated above it and put forward as examples for others to follow and were not excluded from power and influence by it.[67] Régnier-Bohler points out, "Given the anxiety of the ecclesiastical authorities at the desire of women to speak out in public, to proclaim the holy word without intermediary, the linguistic vigor that one finds in spiritual and mystical texts by women is astonishing. There are few if any areas in which women did not express their desire to speak."[68] These women were simply following the prominent examples provided for them by the clergy in the collections of hagiography. The speech exhibited by the female saints sets a precedent that many women in the Middle Ages sought to emulate. Even the saints whose sanctity is measured in silence provide a strong example because they take control over their own destinies and determine the course of their lives and salvation. Just as women were instrumental in the foundation of the early Church, which is the subject of these female saints' lives, they were active in the furtherance of this work during the Middle Ages through example. The manuscripts and collections of hagiography preserve this tradition. TCD MS 319, with the *Gilte Legende*, paints a picture, albeit shady and somewhat incomplete, of how these works may have survived the centuries in the libraries of women who encouraged their reproduction, compilation, and transmission.

These two works were mainstays in libraries across England, and,

66 Ferrante, *To the Glory of Her Sex*, p. 39.
67 Ferrante, *To the Glory of Her Sex*, p. 5.
68 Régnier-Bohler, "Literary and Mystical Voices," p. 433.

in the case of the *Legenda Aurea*, across Europe. They followed the tradition of the early Christian Fathers who wrote extensively on the role of women in religion and society. The female saints were venerated by Jacobus de Voragine, his Middle English successor, and Bokenham in their collections: vocal, rebellious virgin saints such as Dorothy, Margaret of Antioch, etc., who were models not only of chastity and virginity but of power and defiance. They were not expected to remain silent in the face of their persecution and so ordinary medieval women presented with these examples must have been expected to follow them. The impact of these legends is evident in the number of texts written by women, including Julian of Norwich, Margery Kempe, Christine de Pizan, and Hildegard of Bingen, among many others; and in the number of texts written specifically for women as a separate audience that have survived the ravages of time.

Hagiography and literature profoundly shaped and influenced the lives of medieval women in a variety of ways. The existence of texts written for women and about women, even if their original intent was to provide examples of obedience and submission, has had a liberating effect on modern perceptions of the medieval society. As Warner points out,

> It is crucial to remember that, in spite of the misogyny that underpins the Christian religion, it offered women a revolution, as long as they subscribed to its precepts. The early Church offered brotherhood to all men and women, in a manner unknown in the world of antiquity. Although it considered women socially subject to the male, it granted them an identical immortal soul.[69]

Even if the motivation of the original authors was to subjugate women by tainting their sex, they still empower these women to choose for themselves and determine their own fate. As Chaucer's Wife of Bath explains in her tale, "Wommen desire to have sovereynetee/ As well over her housbond as her love,/ And for to been in maistrie him above."[70] Christine de Pizan uses a number of female saints to illustrate her argument against the patristic writers whose work was so widespread. Just as saints like Dorothy or Christina challenge their persecutors and executioners, Christine de Pizan

69 Warner, *Alone of All Her Sex*, p. 72.

70 Geoffrey Chaucer, *The Wife of Bath's Tale*, ed. Peter Beidler (Boston: Bedford/ St Martin's Press, 1996) lines 1038–40.

challenges the men who sought to keep women subservient: "In spite of the slanderer, there are so many good and beautiful women among the ranks of countesses, baronesses, ladies, maidens, bourgeois women, and all classes that God should be praised who upholds them all."[71] There were certainly anti-feminist authors: Saint Jerome claimed that women caused men's judgment to fly away;[72] Saint Ambrose said women were "too inferior in steadfastness for preaching";[73] Saint Augustine insisted that women remain subservient to men;[74] and Abelard said religious houses should be ruled by men because women were incapable and their leadership led to "evil desires in proportion to their dominance."[75] Women were not on equal footing with men in many aspects of society, but these legends reveal that not all women were expected to follow Saint Paul's edict and remain silent in their faith. Women were "dangerous too because of [their] charismatic and prophetic powers of speech, which reflected, from the thirteenth century on, female claims to a new relation with the sacred."[76] The four different categories of female saints show the diversity of women and how their biographers, while embellishing their stories for entertainment value, were not interested in casting them all in one monotonous, submissive light, or confining them to an expected social role.

Ashton criticizes the collection of the *Golden Legend* compiled and printed by William Caxton in 1483 as simplistic and repetitive in its identification of the women in the legends, focusing only on the holy: "Certainly, the female subjects of these tales are reduced to powerless mirror images of patriarchal assumption where the only semi-autonomous existence granted to them is associated purely with the holy."[77] However, the older versions in the *Gilte Legende* do not diminish their early Christian subjects to merely being holy mouthpieces for a masculine pen. If the goal was to relegate women to this position then why let them speak at all? Why give them a

71 Christine de Pizan, *The Book of the City of Ladies*, II.68.11, p. 214.

72 Saint Jerome, *Adversus Jovinianum*, quoted in Blamires, *Woman Defamed and Woman Defended*, p. 65.

73 Saint Ambrose, *Expositio Evangelii Secundum Lucam*, quoted in Blamires, *Woman Defamed and Woman Defended*, p. 62.

74 Saint Augustine, *De Genesi ad Litteram*, quoted in Blamires, *Woman Defamed and Woman Defended*, p. 80.

75 Abelard, *Historia Calamitatum*, quoted in Blamires, *Woman Defamed and Woman Defended*, p. 91.

76 Régnier-Bohler, "Literary and Mystical Voices," p. 429.

77 Ashton, *The Generation of Identity*, p. 41.

voice? Ashton notes that there are two voices in these hagiographies: that of the male authors and that of the women themselves.[78] Christine de Pizan obviously saw these legends as edifying the role of women rather than diminishing it, and her use of the legends to make a case for strong, educated, and vocal women in the face of masculine censure and condemnation shows exactly how influential these legends were for medieval women. Some of the women fit into the mold described by Ashton: saints like Elizabeth of Hungary, who prostrated themselves not only before their God but before the men into whose hands they gave their lives, existence, and souls. Many of these women were saints despite the fact that violent defiance and martyrdom were not an option. Their legends, like those of the mute transvestites, may have been included in the collections of hagiography to illustrate the diversity of religious women, allowing women to choose their role models based on their own situation, and showing that while their faith is the same, the manifestations of it are not and that real women are no more homogeneous than are those of legend. Emilie Amt's examples in *Women's Lives in Medieval Europe* show the extent to which women were active and productive in society.[79] This collection of primary sources illustrates how some expectations for medieval women were idealized, highlighted by many of the legends of female saints. Historical accounts contain instructions for the noble and domestic wives, religious women, and women outside of society: Jews, Muslims, heretics, and sinful women. There was a great deal of material devoted to women as an audience for their education and edification, however unrealistic their proscriptions. Saints' lives served the same function: stories created with an agenda that varied from author to scribe and compiler. Their purpose was manifold: example, entertainment, education, and, perhaps in many ways, a tool of authority. Like Chaucer's works and those of Christine de Pizan, the legends of women saints were widely read and widely circulated. Women were encouraged to read them and emulate their heroines, even if they were brash, independent, and outspoken. The active role of women saints served as a model, and their voice was their form of expression, even if men preserved their words. In some cases their silence speaks for them; they decide their own destiny, often in the face of social

78 Ashton, *The Generation of Identity*, p. 3.

79 Emilie Amt, *Women's Lives in Medieval Europe: A Sourcebook* (New York: Routledge, 1993).

opposition. Despite the position women have occupied in the margins of modern perception of the medieval period, the literature itself tells quite a different story and illuminates the possibilities for women in the Middle Ages through the examples of the women in the *Gilte Legende.*

Select Bibliography

Primary Manuscript Sources

Bodleian Library MS Eng.theo.e.17, Oxford.

This small manuscript is in remarkably good condition, though it is missing its first folio. It only contains *Saint Dorothy* and does not appear to have included anything else or to have been part of a larger collection.

British Library MS Harley 630, folios 154v–168v, London.

This is a fifteenth-century manuscript collection of the *Gilte Legende*, in fairly good condition with no illumination. It includes the entire corpus of the *Gilte Legende* and is one of eleven extant *Gilte Legende* manuscripts.

Trinity College, Dublin Library MS 319.

A badly battered book, this manuscript dates from the fifteenth century and contains two separate fragments of saints' lives: one incomplete section of the *Gilte Legende* and one section with anonymous versions of *Saint Dorothy* and *Saint Catherine*.

Primary Sources and Reference Works

Acta Sanctorum: *Acta sanctorum quotquot toto orbe coluntur*, 3rd edition. Paris: published by the Bollandists, 1863–87.

This is an extensive collection of hagiography in Latin detailing "the Acts of the Saints."

Amt, Emilie. *Women's Lives in Medieval Europe: A Sourcebook.* New York: Routledge, 1993.

An examination of the social and political culture of women in Europe throughout the Middle Ages including their daily routines and roles in society at large. This text provides a comprehensive look at each society and the position of women in it.

Apocryphal Old Testament. Edited by H. F. D. Sparks. Oxford: Clarendon Press, 1984.

This is a comprehensive edition of the texts of the Old Testament apocrypha translated with notes and commentary.

"Announcement to the Three Marys, Peter and John at the Sepulchre: Play 36." In *N-Town Cycle, Cotton MS Vespasian D8*. Edited by Stephen Spector. Early English Text Society, supplementary series 11, Oxford: Oxford University Press, 1991.

A modern translation and edition of the popular medieval version of the biblical story about the announcement at the tomb of Christ after the Crucifixion, where Mary Magdalene is given the command to spread the news of Christ's Resurrection. Complete with notes and introduction.

"Appearance to Mary Magdalene: Play 37." In *N-Town Cycle, Cotton MS Vespasian D8*. Edited by Stephen Spector. Early English Text Society, supplementary series 11, Oxford: Oxford University Press, 1991.

Another play in the N-town cycle highlighting Mary Magdalene's role in spreading the word of the Resurrection. Full transcription with notes and introduction.

Barratt, Alexandra. *A Commentary on the Penitential Psalms Translated by Dame Eleanor Hull*. Early English Text Society, original series 307. Oxford: Oxford University Press, 1995.

This is an edition of the psalms translated by Dame Eleanor Hull as well as extended commentary on her life, her work, and her impact on the transmission of popular religious texts.

Blamires, Alcuin. *Woman Defamed and Woman Defended: An Anthology of Medieval Texts*. Oxford: Clarendon Press, 1992.

A collection of antifeminist works ranging from the early Greek philosophers, early Church Fathers, and late-medieval clerics set against contemporary medieval works defending women, their independence, and their position in society by such authors as Geoffrey Chaucer and Christine de Pizan. Blamires includes works by Aristotle, Abelard, Saint Paul, and many others. Unfortunately, the section on antifeminist works is much longer then the section defending women, but it is a comprehensive edition nonetheless.

Bokenham, Osbern. *Legends of Holy Women: A Translation of Osbern Bokenham's "Legendys of Hooly Wummen."* Edited by Sheila Delany. Notre Dame, Ind.: University of Notre Dame Press, 1992.

A modern translation of Bokenham's collection of female saints' lives, with commentary and analysis on the origins of the text and his audience.

———. *Legendys of Hooly Wummen*. Edited by Mary Serjeantson. Early English Text Society, original series 206. Oxford: Oxford University Press, 1938.

An edition in Middle English of Bokenham's collection of female saints' lives, including commentary on his sources, and the transmission of his texts.

Butler, Alban. *Butler's Lives of Saints*. New York: P. J. Kennedy and Sons, 1963.

A modern collection of saints' lives given in liturgical sequence and taken from medieval texts. This edition gives a synopsis of each saint and a description of their cults and legends.

Chaucer, Geoffrey. *The Wife of Bath's Tale*. Edited by Peter Beidler. Boston: Bedford/St Martin's Press, 1996.

A critical edition of Chaucer's *Wife of Bath's Prologue and Tale* with the full text in Middle English of this story from the *Canterbury Tales*.

Chester Cycle, The. "Resurrection: The Skinners Play or Play 18." Edited by R. M. Lumiansky and David Mills. Early English Text Society, supplementary series 3. Oxford: Oxford University Press, 1974.

An edition of the Chester Cycle of medieval mystery plays presented with commentary and analysis of staging and performance.

Christine de Pizan. *The Book of the City of Ladies*. Translated by Earl Jeffrey Richards. New York: Persea Books, 1998.

Written in the fourteenth century, this is an answer to the works of antifeminist clerics – including Saint Augustine's *City of God* – where the true virtues of women are explored through a number of legends, tales, and commentary.

Cruden, Alexander. *Cruden's Complete Concordance to the Old and New Testaments*. London: Lutterworth Press, 1941.

A guide to finding key phrases and verses in the Old and New Testament of the Latin Vulgate in English.

Donovan, Leslie. *Women Saints' Lives in Old English Prose*. Cambridge: D. S. Brewer, 1999.

A modern English translation of female saints' lives in Anglo-Saxon manuscripts of the *Golden Legend* including Saints Lucy, Eugenia, and Agatha, among others. Each legend is preceded by a commentary about the history and spread of the saint's life and cult.

Duchet-Suchaux, Gaston, and Michel Pastoureau. *The Bible and the Saints*. New York: Flammarion, 1994.

An alphabetical guide to saints and their iconography, including the origin of each saint and a brief synopsis of his or her popular legend.

Dutripon, Francois Pascal. *Concordantiae Bibliorum Sacrorum Vulgatae Editionis*. Paris: Belin-Mander, 1838.

A concordance, in Latin, to the text of the Latin Vulgate Bible.

English Mystery Plays. Edited by Peter Happe. London: Penguin English Library, 1975.

A collection of Middle English mystery plays, in translation, popularly performed on feast days and during religious celebrations, including an introduction and notes.

Farmer, David Hugh. *Oxford Dictionary of Saints*. Oxford: Oxford University Press, 1978.

A comprehensive dictionary of saints, listed alphabetically, and designed as a quick reference guide to the properties and legends of saints.

Hamer, Richard. *Three Lives from the "Gilte Legende" edited from MS BL Egerton 876*. Heidelberg: Universitätsverlag Carl Winter, 1978.

This is Hamer's first study on the *Gilte Legende* and is composed of a critical edition of three male saints' legends, commentary, and analysis on the origin of the Middle English version of the Latin *Legenda Aurea,* as well as authorial possibilities. Hamer compares textual and linguistic evidence and proposes Saint Albans monastery as the possible place of composition for the original *Gilte Legende.*

Hamer, Richard and Vida Russell. *Supplementary Lives in Some Manuscripts of the "Gilte Legende."* Early English Text Society, original series 315. Oxford: Oxford University Press, 2000.

A comprehensive critical edition of all the supplementary lives included in manuscripts of the *Gilte Legende* but not part of the original corpus of lives from the *Golden Legend*. Each life is transcribed and compared to texts in other *Gilte Legende* manuscripts, including early Anglo-Saxon lives translationed by the scribe into Middle English, specific local saints, and the three versions of the *Life of Saint Dorothy*. In the introduction, Hamer discusses the relationship of the various manuscripts, their composition, and their transmission.

Holy Bible, Douay-Rheims version. Revised by Bishop Richard Challoner, 1749–52.

A modern English translation of the Latin Vulgate Bible compiled at Douay and Rheims by Saint Jerome in the fourth century.

Jacobus de Voragine. *The Golden Legend*. Edited by Christopher Stace with an introduction by Richard Hamer. Middlesex: Penguin Books, 1998.

The translation of excerpts from the Latin *Golden Legend* originally written by Jacobus de Voragine circa 1260. This is one of the most popular texts of the Middle Ages and was translated into numerous vernaculars and disseminated all over Europe.

———. *The Golden Legend: Readings on the Saints*. Translated and edited by William Granger Ryan. 2 vols. Princeton: Princeton University Press, 1993.

The first complete translation in modern English of Jacobus de Voragine's *Legenda Aurea*, with notes.

Langland, William. *The Vision of Piers Plowman: A Critical Edition of the B-Text Based on Trinity College Cambridge MS B.15.17*. Edited by A. V. C. Schmidt. London: Everyman Press, 1995.

A translation and edition of Langland's *Piers Plowman*, a moral poem about living a good and virtuous life, complete with introduction and commentary.

Linguistic Atlas of Late Medieval English. Edited by Angus McIntosh, M. L. Samuels, Michael Benskin, et al. Aberdeen: University of Aberdeen Press, 1986

A comprehensive study of the linguistic dialect used in English literature during the Middle Ages, pinpointing the origin of texts based on spelling and pronunciation.

Lives of Women Saints of our Contrie of England. Edited by C. Horstmann. Early English Text Society, original series 86. Oxford: Oxford University Press, 1998.

This 1888 edition of women saints' lives was the original, definitive collection on the subject. Horstmann's ideas and theories regarding the Middle English hagiographical collections, including the *Gilte Legende*, shaped the field for more than seventy years and influenced almost every scholar of hagiography who succeeded him.

"Mary Magdalen." In *Late Medieval Religious Plays of Bodleian MSS Digby 133 and E Museo 160*. Edited by Donald C. Baker, John L. Murphy, and Louis B. Hall Jr. Early English Text Society, original series 283. Oxford: Oxford University Press, 1982.

A critical Middle English edition of the Digby version of "Mary Magdalene," an apocryphal account of the saint's life, her history, her relationship with Christ, and her role as a preacher in Marseilles. This story is very similar to that found in the *Gilte Legende* account of Mary Magdalene.

Middle English Dictionary. Edited by Hans Kurath et al. Ann Arbor, Mich.: University of Michigan Press, 1956.

The incomplete dictionary of Middle English compiled from the occurrence of words in Middle English texts.

New Catholic Encyclopedia. Edited by the staff at Catholic University, Washington, D.C. New York: McGraw-Hill Book Company, 1967.

The full encyclopedia of Catholic knowledge ranging from saints and sinners, to practice and places, and doctrine and heresy.

New Testament Apocrypha. Edited by Edgar Hennecke and Wilhelm Schneemelcher. London: Lutterworth Press, 1963.

An edition of the apocryphal texts of the New Testament in translation with notes, introduction, and commentary on the origins of apocrypha and the implications of their existence. This edition includes the *Gospel of Mary Magdalene* and discusses the origins of this text and its place in later biblical tradition.

Oxford Dictionary of English Etymology. Edited by C. T. Onions. Oxford: Clarendon Press, 1966.

The complete dictionary on the origins of words and their use in modern English.

Pagels, Elaine. *The Gnostic Gospels*. New York: Vintage Books, 1979.

An edition and translation of a number of texts from the apocryphal Gnostic gospels, including analysis and commentary on the impact these texts had on medieval society and the religion of the Catholic Church.

Patrologia Latina. Edited by J. P. Migne. Paris: D'Ambrose, 1844–55.

The comprehensive compilation of early Latin texts by the Church Fathers and early Christian biographers, including Saint Jerome, Saint

Augustine, and Saint Paul. Some of the texts are included in their entirety in Latin.

Thiebaux, Marcelle. *The Writings of Medieval Women: An Anthology.* New York: Garland Publishing, 1994.
A comprehensive anthology of writing by women in the Middle Ages; from secular stories to saintly revelations, this anthology provides a compendium of works written by women, for women, including the work of Hildegard of Bingen and Christine de Pizan.

White, Hugh, translator and editor. *Ancrene Wisse: Guide for Anchoresses*. London: Penguin Books, 1993.
A translation in modern English of the thirteenth-century guide for anchoresses detailing the obligations of these holy women and the rules they must follow to lead a pure and sanctified life.

Winstead, Karen. *Chaste Passions: Medieval English Virgin Martyr Legends*. Ithaca: Cornell University Press, 2000.
A collection of legends by a host of medieval authors, including Geoffrey Chaucer and Osbern Bokenham, focusing on female saints. Taken from a number of medieval collections like the *South English Legendary*, the *Scottish Legendary*, and the *North English Legendary.*

Secondary Sources

Abou-El-Haj, Barbara. *The Medieval Cult of Saints: Formations and Transformations*. Cambridge: Cambridge University Press, 1997.
An examination of the proliferation of saints' cults, primarily in eleventh- and twelfth-century Europe, including cult practices, especially in visual art. Her work focuses mainly on the cult of Saint Amand and its spread and iconography. However, she addresses the portrayal of saints and their cults as a medieval phenomenon not restricted to any one culture or society.

Alexandre, Monique. "Early Christian Women." In *A History of Women in the West, vol. I: From Ancient Goddesses to Christian Saints.* Edited by Pauline Schmitt Pantel. Cambridge: Harvard University Press, 1992. Pp. 409–44.
An examination of the role played by women in the early Christian period and the impact they had on the foundation of culture and religion. Alexandre discusses the dichotomy of the Church's position regarding women and the specific place of women among the ranks of early Christian saints.

Ashton, Gail. *The Generation of Identity in Late Medieval Hagiography: Speaking the Saint*. London: Routledge, 2000.

This study focuses on the depiction and portrayal of female saints. Ashton examines the controlling voice of male biographers and the "subversive female voice" that comes through in the legends of the female martyrs. Ashton includes excerpts from Bokenham's *Legendys of Hooly Wummen* and *The Golden Legend*.

Bell, Susan Groag. "Medieval Women Book Owners: Arbiters of Lay Piety and Ambassadors of Culture." In *Women and Power in the Middle Ages*. Edited by Mary Erler and Maryanne Kowaleski. Athens: University of Georgia Press, 1988.

This essay is part of a collection of articles analyzing the role of women in medieval society. Bell focuses on the importance of women in the literary culture of the Middle Ages, specifically their role as book owners and keepers of knowledge.

Blamires, Alcuin. "Women and Preaching in Medieval Orthodoxy, Heresy, and Saints' Lives," *Viator* 26 (1995): 135–52.

Blamires discusses the position of women preachers in religious texts, and analyzes the implication of their voice both inside and outside the doctrine of the medieval Church.

Brownlee, Kevin. "Martyrdom and the Female Voice: Saint Christine in the *Cite des Dames*." In *Images of Sainthood in Medieval Europe*. Edited by Renate Blumenfeld-Kosinski and Timea K. Szell. Ithaca: Cornell University Press, 1991.

Brownlee takes a close look at the life and legend of Saint Christina included in Christine de Pizan's *Cite des Dames*, analyzing her powerful speech and its significance in female hagiography and Christine de Pizan's work.

Bynum, Caroline Walker. *Holy Feast and Holy Fast: the Religious Significance of Food to Medieval Women*. Berkeley and London: University of California Press, 1987.

In this groundbreaking work, Walker Bynum discusses the trend of "holy anorexia" and its representation in hagiography and the religious culture of the Middle Ages, as well as the significance of heavenly manna and other holy feasts.

———. *Fragmentation and Redemption: Essays on Gender and the Human Body in Medieval Religion*. New York: Zone Books, 1992.

This collection of essays, edited by Walker Bynum, focuses on the representations and use of the body in religious texts, and how gender determined social roles and religious piety.

Cartlidge, Neil. *Medieval Marriage: Literary Approaches, 1100–1300.* Cambridge: D. S. Brewer, 1997.

An examination of literary accounts of marriage, and the misperception that marriage was merely a social convention and political tool employed without feeling or emotion. Cartlidge illustrates that love was very much a part of medieval marriage and that marriage in the Middle ages was a complex institution.

Casagrande, Carla. "The Protected Woman." In Klapisch-Zuber. Pp. 70–104.

This article focuses on the diverse role of women in Western medieval society and how women were venerated as objects of purity, like the Virgin Mary, or despised as objects of disgust, like Eve. Casagrande also examines the reverence for Mary Magdalene and her position as both a sinner and a saint.

Coletti, Teresa. "Paupertas est donum Dei: Hagiography, Lay Religion, and the Economics of Salvation in the Digby *Mary Magdalene*." *Speculum* Vol. 76, no. 2 (2001): 337–78.

A comprehensive study of the Digby *Mary Magdalene* and its influence on the social and economic culture of the Middle Ages.

Dalarun, Jacques. "The Clerical Gaze." In Klapisch-Zuber. Pp. 15–42.

An examination of how the history of women was filtered through the gaze and perceptions of male clerics who focused on their relation to Eve and what they considered the inherent flaws of women. Dalarun also discusses the origins of the Magdalene legend and its influence on medieval culture.

Davis, Natalie Zemon. Foreword to *The Book of the City of Ladies* by Christine de Pizan, translated by Earl Jeffery Richards. New York: Persea Books, 1998.

The foreword to this modern English translation introduces questions of culture and content in the work of Christine de Pizan.

Driver, Martha. "Mirrors of a Collective Past: Reconsidering Images of Medieval Women." In *Women and the Book: Assessing the Visual Evidence.* Edited by Lesley Smith. London: British Library, 1997. Pp. 75–93.

A new look at the iconography and representation of women in medieval art, particularly book illuminations. Driver discusses the role of women in book production and dissemination as well as their greater role in medieval society.

Duby, Georges and Michelle Perrot. "Writing the History of Women." In *A History of Women in the West, vol. I: Ancient Goddesses to Christian Saints*. Edited by Pauline Schmitt Pantel. Cambridge, Mass.: Harvard University Press, 1992. Pp. ix–xxi.

This essay, written by the general editors as a preface to the series on the history of women in the West, examines the role of women in history and their presence in the historical record.

Duffy, Eamon. *Stripping of the Altars*. New Haven: Yale University Press, 1992.

A striking study of the detrimental effects of the Reformation on a "popular and theologically respectable religious system" that was the medieval Catholic Church, and how this institution was laid bare in the sixteenth century.

Dutton, Anne. "Passing the Book: Testamentary Transmission of Religious Literature to and by Women in England, 1350–1500." In *Women, the Book, and the Godly*. Edited by Lesley Smith and Jane H. M. Taylor. Cambridge: D. S. Brewer, 1995.

A focused look on the tradition of literary transmission of religious texts in England during the height of the medieval period, and the part played by women in disseminating those texts.

Edwards, A. S. G. "The Transmission and Audience of Osbern Bokenham's *Legendys of Hooly Wummen*." In *Late Medieval Religious Texts and Their Transmission*. Edited by A. J. Minnis. Cambridge: D. S. Brewer, 1994.

This article focuses on identifying the audience for Bokenham's *Legendys of Hooly Wummen*, analyzing his sources and the transmission of manuscripts containing his work. Edwards puts forward some suggestions about the origin of the version of the *Dorothy* legend found in Bokenham as well as suggestions regarding the authorship of the *Gilte Legende*.

Eliade, Mircea. *The Sacred and the Profane: The Nature of Religion*. San Diego, Calif.: Harcourt/Brace & Co., 1959.

An introduction to the history of religion, primarily the various manifestations of faith and sacred belief, including early Christianity, paganism, and Judaism. Eliade also discusses the diverse interpretations of religious belief that shaped religious thought in the Middle Ages.

Elliott, Dyan. "Dress as mediator Between Inner and Outer Self: the Pious Matron of the High and Later Middle Ages." *Mediaeval Studies* 53 (1991): 279–308.

A focused analysis of how dress served as a reflection of internal piety and devotion, specifically among matrons of the later Middle Ages.

Fein, Susanna. "A Saint 'Geynest under Gore': Marina and the Love Lyrics of the Seventh Quire." In *Studies in the Harley Manuscript: The Scribes, Contents, and Scribal Contexts of British Library MS Harley 2253*. Edited by Fein. Kalamazoo, Mich.: Medieval Institute Publications, 2000.

The full volume is an edition of the collection in Harley MS 2253. However, Fein's article discusses the legend of Saint Marina found in the manuscript and compares the implications of her gender switch to the lewd language used in the love lyrics.

Ferrante, Joan M. *To the Glory of Her Sex: Women's Roles in the Composition of Medieval Texts*. Bloomington and Indianapolis: Indiana University Press, 1997.

An exploration of the role of women in the composition and dissemination of medieval texts, including independent writers like Marie de France and Christine de Pizan. Ferrante challenges the notion that book composition was exclusively carried out by male scribes and authors.

Finke, Laurie. *Women's Writing in English: Medieval England*. London: Longman Publishing, 1999.

A look at the influence of women authors on medieval literature, specifically in English, and the impact their work had on English culture.

Görlach, Manfred. *The "South English Legendary", "Gilte Legende" and "Golden Legend"*. Braunschweig: Institut fur Anglistik und Amerikanistik, 1972.

An extensive study of the provenance and history of hagiography, specifically these Middle English collections. Görlach also examines the connections between these medieval texts.

———. *Studies in Middle English Saints' Legends*. Heidelberg: Universitätsverlag Carl Winter, 1998

A summary of thirty years of Görlach's work on Middle English legendaries.

Hanna, Ralph. "Some Norfolk Women and Their Books." In *The Cultural Patronage of Medieval Women*. Edited by June Hall McCash. Athens: University of Georgia Press, 1996.

A detailed study of women book owners in Norfolk, England, and the contribution made by women to the literary culture of the Middle Ages.

Heffernan, Thomas J. *Sacred Biography: Saints and Their Biographies in the Middle Ages*. Oxford: Oxford University Press, 1989.

A discussion of hagiography and its impact on medieval culture, society, and religious ideology.

Holdsworth, Christopher. "Hermits and the Power of the Frontier." *Reading Medieval Studies* 16 (1990): 55–76.

A discussion of the social function of anchorites and recluses, and their influence on medieval society and religious traditions.

Hopkins, Andrea. *Most Wise and Valiant Ladies: Remarkable Lives of Women of the Middle Ages*. Oxford: Collins & Brown, 1997.

A collection of accounts about the lives of remarkable medieval women who rose to prominence in their own time and have been venerated throughout history for their strength, power, and determination, including Christine de Pizan and Eleanor of Aquitaine.

Jansen, Katherine Ludwig. *The Making of the Magdalen: Preaching and Popular Devotion in the Later Middle Ages*. Princeton: Princeton University Press, 2000.

A complete history of the invention and origin of the Mary Magdalen legend, including her biblical tradition and the apocryphal texts that sprang up around her cult, making her one of the most popular saints – second only to the Virgin Mary.

Jeremy, Sister Mary. "Caxton and the Synfulle Wretche." *Traditio* 4 (1946): 423–8.

This article examines the evidence for authorship in the *Gilte Legende* manuscripts, including a colophon attributing the collection to a "synfulle wretche" and the suggestion that William Caxton may have used one of the Middle English manuscripts of the *Gilte Legende* when compiling his translation of the *Golden Legend*.

Kelly, Kathleen Coyne. *Performing Virginity and Testing Chastity in the Middle Ages*. London: Routledge, 2000.
An analysis of female virginity in the Middle Ages through a variety of texts, including medical treatises, and historical and legal documents, but the main focus is the representation of virgins in hagiography.

Klapisch-Zuber, Christiane, ed. *A History of Women in the West, vol. II: Silences of the Middle Ages*. Cambridge, Mass.: Belknap Press of Harvard University Press, 1992.
This comprehensive collection of essays examines the diversity of women in Middle Ages and their roles in society, focusing on picking out a female voice from among the records of history.

Kurvinen, Auvo. "Caxton's *Golden Legend* and the *Gilte Legende*." *Neuphilologische Mitteilungen* 3 (1959): 353–75.
Kurvinen picks up where Jeremy left off, making a case for Caxton's use of British Library MS 35298 as the Middle English exemplar for his printed edition of the *Golden Legend*.

Larrington, Carolyne. *Women and Writing in Medieval Europe*. London: Routledge, 1995.
An examination of the role of women in the composition of texts and the impact women had on medieval European culture through their ownership of books and their authorship. Larrington suggests that women played a much more active role in the literacy of their time than has been previously assumed.

Lewis, Katherine J. *The Cult of St. Katherine of Alexandria in Late-Medieval England*. Woodbridge: Boydell Press, 2000.
A detailed discussion and analysis of Saint Katherine's cult and the influence it had on religion in England, especially for women.

———. " 'Lete me suffre': Reading the Torture of St. Margaret of Antioch in Late-Medieval England." In *Medieval Women: Texts and Contexts in Late-Medieval Britain: Essays for Felicity Riddy*. Edited by Jocelyn Wogan-Browne et al. Turnhout, Belgium: Brepols, 2000.
A discussion of the use of torture in female hagiography, specifically the life of Margaret of Antioch, and the implications of sexualized torture in women saints' lives.

———. "Model Girls? Virgin Martyrs and the Training of Young Medieval Women in Late Medieval England." In *Young Medieval Women*. Edited by Katherine Lewis, Noel James Menuge, and Kim Phillips. Gloucester: Sutton, 1999.

An analysis of the influence virgin-martyr legends had on young women in the Middle Ages, and what kind of example they provided.

Leyser, Henrietta. *Medieval Women: A Social History of Women in England, 450–1500*. London: Phoenix Grant, 1995.

This study looks at the diverse roles of women in medieval English society and how they influenced society through their traditional positions of homemaker, business manager, and mother.

L'Hermite-Ledercq, Paulette. "The Feudal Order." In Klapisch-Zuber. Pp. 202–49.

This article focuses on effects of the feudal order in medieval society, and women's place within the political structure.

McInerney, Maud Burnett. "Rhetoric, Power, and Integrity in the Passion of the Virgin Martyr." In *Menacing Virgins: Representing Virginity in the Middle Ages and Renaissance*. Edited by Kathleen Coyne Kelly and Marina Leslie. Newark, N.J.: University of Delaware Press, 1999. Pp. 50–70.

A detailed study of the power wielded by virgin martyrs, especially through their vocal defiance, and the influence their legends had on medieval women and the medieval concept of women in religion.

Meek, C. E. and M. K. Simms. *"The Fragility of Her Sex?": Medieval Irish Women in Their European Context*. Dublin: Four Courts Press, 1996.

This collection of essays examines the role of women in medieval society and challenges the notion of female fragility, as well as drawing parallels between the women of medieval Ireland and the rest of Europe.

Mooney, Catherine. *Gendered Voices: Medieval Saints and Their Interpreters*. Edited by Mooney. Philadelphia: University of Pennsylvania Press, 1999.

This is a multi-authored collection of essays examining the voices of female saints as heard through their male biographers. The contributors separate those voices in an attempt to find the true voice of these women free from the censure and interpretation of male clerics.

Moore, Samuel. "Patrons of Letters in Norfolk and Suffolk c. 1450." *Publications of the Modern Language Association of America.* Vol. XXVII (1912): 188–200.

A study of the epistolary tradition in Norfolk and Suffolk, including the presence of women. Moore examines the history, provenance, and content of a series of personal letters.

Mulder-Bakker, Anneke B., ed. *Sanctity and Motherhood: Essays on Holy Mothers in the Middle Ages*. New York: Garland, 1995.

A collection of essays dedicated to the representation of motherhood in medieval Christianity and the role of mothers in hagiography.

Newman, Barbara. *From Virile Woman to WomanChrist*. Philadelphia, Pa.: University of Pennsylvania Press, 1995.

A critical study of the role of women in medieval Christianity and how their position changed through the centuries. The chapter "Maternal Martyrs" gives a detailed analysis of mothers as martyrs in hagiography and the representation of motherhood in medieval religious texts.

Peterson, Joan. *Handmaids of the Lord: Holy Women in Late Antiquity and the Early Middle Ages*. Kalamazoo, Mich.: Cistercian Publications, 1996.

An examination of the role of women in religion in the earliest Christian centuries and the early Middle Ages and how that role changed as Christianity became the accepted religion of the Western empire.

Phillips, Kim. "Maidenhood as the Perfect Age of Woman's Life." In *Young Medieval Women*. Edited by Katherine Lewis, James Menuge, and Kim Phillips. Gloucester: Sutton, 1999.

A discussion of the "perfect age" ascribed to young virgins, usually fourteen or fifteen, when they reach their spiritual awareness, and the representations of this in medieval religious texts.

Quilligan, Maureen. *The Allegory of Female Authority: Christine de Pisan's "Cite des Dames."* Ithaca: Cornell University Press, 1991.

Quilligan examines the importance of Christine de Pizan's work as a representation of female authority and her challenge of the patristic authority wielded by her contemporary male authors.

Reames, Sherry L. *The* Legenda Aurea*: A Re-Examination of its Paradoxical History*. Madison, Wisc., and London: University of Wisconsin Press, 1985.

A new look at Jacobus's compilation of hagiography, and an examination of its contradictions.

Régnier-Bohler, Danielle. "Literary and Mystical Voices." In Klapisch-Zuber. Pp. 427–82.

An examination of women's presence in medieval texts, both religious and secular, and the importance of female expression despite male opposition.

Riddy, Felicity. "Women Talking about the Things of God: a Late Medieval Sub-Culture." In *Women and Literature in Britain, 1150–1500*. Edited by Carol M. Meale. Cambridge: Cambridge University Press, 1993.

Riddy examines the vocal subculture of women involved in the dissemination and discussion of religious texts in medieval England.

Salih, Sarah. "Performing Virginity: Sex and Violence in the Katherine Group." In *Constructions of Widowhood and Virginity in the Middle Ages*. Edited by Cindy L. Carlson and Angela Jane Weisl. New York: St Martin's Press, 1999.

Part of the continuing debate regarding the sexualization of torture in female hagiography and its uses against virgin martyrs, specifically the Katherine Group.

Sawyer, Deborah. *Women and Religion in the First Christian Centuries*. London: Routledge, 1996.

A comprehensive look at the role of women in the foundation and dissemination of Christianity in its earliest years during the period of Roman imperial rule. Sawyer focuses on the religious functions performed by women and their effect on later Christianity.

Smith, Lesley. "Scriba Femina: Medieval Depictions of Women Writing." In *Women and the Book: Assessing the Visual Evidence*. Edited by Lesley Smith. London: British Library, 1997.

A clear picture of female book ownership and authorship portrayed in medieval illuminations of women holding books, writing them, or reading them, and a detailed analysis of how those images shape the perception of women in the Middle Ages.

Tibbetts Schulenberg, Jane. *Forgetful of Their Sex: Female Sanctity and Society ca. 500–1100*. Chicago: University of Chicago Press, 1998.

A study of how women rose above their prescribed social positions in the Middle Ages to positions of power and influence and how many of these women were venerated by men despite their gender, especially in the realm of medieval hagiography.

———. "The Heroics of Virginity: Brides of Christ and Sacrificial Mutilation." In *Women in the Middle Ages and Renaissance*. Edited by Mary Beth Rose. Syracuse, N.Y.: Syracuse University Press, 1986.

An examination of the role of torture and self-mutilation in the legends of virgin martyrs, and the implications of this form of sacrifice.

———. "Saints' Lives as a Source for the History of Women, 500–1100." In *Medieval Women and the Sources of Medieval History*. Edited by Joel T. Rosenthal. Athens: University of Georgia Press, 1990. Pp. 285–320.

This article examines the usefulness of hagiography as a means of painting a clear, historical picture of women in the Middle Ages. Tibbetts Schulenberg argues that these legends are a rich source of historical material and should not be dismissed as mere fantasy written by men who had their own agenda in reproducing the legends of female saints.

Tracy, Larissa. "British Library MS Harley 630: Saint Alban's and Lydgate." *Journal of the Early Book Society*. Vol. 3. New York: Pace University Press, 2000. Pp. 36–58.

This article examines evidence that suggests John Lydgate used Harley MS 630 as a Middle English exemplar for his *Life of Saint Alban and Saint Amphibal* and addresses the question of ownership and dissemination of the *Gilte Legende*.

Vauchez, André. *Sainthood in the Later Middle Ages*. Translated by Jean Birrell. Cambridge: Cambridge University Press, 1997.

A comprehensive look at the tradition of sainthood in the later Middle Ages, and its influence on medieval society.

Warner, Marina. *Alone of All Her Sex: The Myth and Cult of the Virgin Mary*. New York: Vintage Books, 1976.

A comprehensive study of the varied roles of the Virgin Mary in all facets of literature, art, culture, legend, and history.

Warren, Ann. *Anchorites and Their Patrons in Medieval England.* Berkeley: University of California Press, 1985.

A comprehensive discussion of the anchorite tradition and their function in medieval society.

Weinstein, Donald and Rudolph M. Bell. *Saints and Society: The Two Worlds of Western Christendom, 1000–1700.* Chicago and London: University of Chicago Press, 1982.

Weinstein and Bell provide a comprehensive analysis of the role of hagiography in medieval society and its implications in Western Christianity.

Winstead, Karen. *Virgin Martyrs: Legends of Sainthood in Late Medieval England.* Ithaca: Cornell University Press, 1997.

An examination of virgin-martyr legends of torture and execution and the subtle shift in their representations in late medieval England.

Wogan-Browne, Jocelyn. *Saints' Lives and the Literary Culture of Women, c. 1150–1300: Virginity and its Authorizations.* Oxford: Oxford University Press, 2001.

A comprehensive look at the influence of hagiography on the literary culture of women, specifically the impact of virgin-martyr legends. This study focuses on English martyr legends and illustrates the diverse role of virginity in literature of the twelfth and thirteenth centuries.

Index